Anonymous

A Memorial Volume of the Bi-Centennial Celebration of the Town of Windham, Connecticut

Anonymous

A Memorial Volume of the Bi-Centennial Celebration of the Town of Windham, Connecticut

ISBN/EAN: 9783744715874

Printed in Europe, USA, Canada, Australia, Japan

Cover: Foto ©ninafisch / pixelio.de

More available books at **www.hansebooks.com**

A

MEMORIAL VOLUME

OF THE

BI-CENTENNIAL CELEBRATION

OF THE

TOWN OF WINDHAM, CONNECTICUT.

CONTAINING THE

HISTORICAL ADDRESSES, POEMS, AND A DESCRIPTION OF EVENTS
CONNECTED WITH THE OBSERVANCE OF THE TWO HUNDRETH
ANNIVERSARY OF THE INCORPORATION OF THE
TOWN, AS HELD IN THE YEAR 1892.

Published by the Committee.

HARTFORD, CONN:
THE NEW ENGLAND HOME PRINTING CO.
1893.

WINDHAM GREEN, JUNE 8, 1892.

PRELIMINARY EFFORTS.

In the warning of the annual town meeting of the town of Windham, called for October 5th, 1891, the fifth clause, inserted by the selectmen on request of interested citizens, called upon the town to decide whether it would authorize an appropriation and appoint a committee to provide for the proper celebration of the approaching bi-centennial anniversary, May 12th, 1892. As October 5th was the day of the annual town election, action upon the bi-centennial was postponed one week, or until October 12th. The town records show that on this latter date it was

Voted—That James E. Hayden, John G. Keigwin, Lloyd E. Baldwin, Silas F. Loomer, Edwin E. Burnham, James E. Murray, John M. Hall, Thomas J. Kelley, Everett H Moulton, and E. Clinton Winchester be empowered to nominate a permanent committee consisting of twenty citizens of the town, who are hereby instructed to consider the matter contained in the fifth clause of the warning and devise means for the performance of the same, and report to an early future town meeting.

In accordance with this vote, the nominating committee met October 17th and named as the permanent committee of twenty citizens, the following : John M. Hall, Allen B. Lincoln, Everett H. Moulton, Guilford Smith. James E. Murray, Henry Larrabee, James E. Hayden, Edwin H. Hall, Eugene S. Boss, John G. Keigwin, Charles J Fox, Lloyd E. Baldwin, Joel W. Webb, Silas F. Loomer, Thomas J. Kelley, William C. Jillson, James Walden, John H. Moulton, James T. Lynch, M. Eugene Lincoln

The permanent committee organized October 24th, with Eugene S. Boss as president, Henry Larrabee and James E. Murray as active vice-presidents, Thomas J. Kelley secretary, James Walden treasurer, and M. Eugene Lincoln, John G. Keigwin, Charles J. Fox, John H. Moulton and James Walden as executive committee.

Subsequently, the following list of honorary vice-presidents was announced by the permanent committee:

HONORARY VICE-PRESIDENTS.

Windham.—John Brown, Israel G. Robinson, Hardin H. Fitch, Elisha G. Hammond, Harry Boss, Charles Smith, William Wales, William Swift, Edwin E. Burnham, Waldo Bingham, Jonathan Hatch, Frank M. Lincoln, Albert R. Moulton, John A. Perkins, Henry Page, Joseph B. Bliven, Marvin Burnham, William Moulton, Abner D. Loring, Freeman D. Spencer, Lucius Y. Flint, Jairus Smith, Charles Larrabee, George Lathrop, Chester Tilden, Charles S. Bliven, Rufus Huntington, Edward L. Burnham, Albert L. Perry, Silas F. Clark, Joseph C. Bassett, Henry Spafford, William C. Cargel, Chauncey W. Turner, Albert A. Conant, Lorin Lincoln, Florimond DeBruycker, Benjamin B. Hoxie, William H. Osborn, Norman Meloney, J. Godfrey La Palme, John Hickey, Arthur P. Favroe, Jeremiah O'Sullivan, George W. Burnham, Roderick Davison, Albert Hartson.

Chaplin—David A. Griggs, John R. Utley, Origen Bennett.

Hampton.—Patrick H. Pearl, Linden T. Button, David A. Greenslit, Storrs Swift, Palmer Fenton.

Mansfield.—Augustus Storrs, Lucian Freeman, Henry Starkweather.

Scotland.—William F. Palmer, John P. Gager, Henry Carey.

Julius G. Rathbun, Ward W. Jacobs, Edward S. Cleveland, of Hartford; Horace Winslow, of Simsbury; George H. Chase, of Stamford; William C. Witter of New York.

Following were the permanent and special committees appointed:

PERMANENT COMMITTEE.

Chairman.—Eugene S. Boss.
Active Vice-Presidents.—Henry Larrabee, James E. Murray.
Secretary.—Thomas J. Kelley.
Treasurer.—James Walden.
Executive Committee.—M. Eugene Lincoln, John G. Keigwin, Charles J. Fox, John H. Moulton, James Walden.
Other Members:—John M. Hall, Allen B. Lincoln, Everett H. Moulton, Guilford Smith, Edwin H. Hall, Lloyd E. Baldwin, Joel W. Webb, Silas F. Loomer, William C. Jillson, James T. Lynch.

SPECIAL COMMITTEES.

Finance.—James Walden, J. Griffin Martin, Horace M. Chapman, Jeremiah O'Sullivan, Guilford Smith, E. Harlow Holmes, Henry Larrabee, Frank F. Webb, Edwin H. Hall, George T. Spafford, Theodore Potvin, J. Calhoun Bugbee.

Reception.—Eugene S. Boss, Julius Pinney, Oliver H. K. Risley, John L. Hunter, Arthur S. Winchester, Lucius J. Hammond.

Oration.—Elliott B. Sumner, George W. Meloney, T. Morton Hills, Charles H. Colgrove, William Swift.

History.—Edwin A. Buck, Waldo Bingham, Frank M. Lincoln, Frank M. Wilson, James T. Lynch.

Relics.—Horatio N. Bill, George Challenger, Charles Larrabee, George Lathrop.

Abel E. Brooks of Hartford, Joseph B. Merrow of Mansfield, Edgar S. Lincoln of Chaplin, Roger Williams of Hampton, Rufus T. Haskins of Scotland.

Industrial Exhibit.—John Scott, Albert R. Morrison, Samuel L. Burlingham, J. Dwight Chaffee, Thomas C. Chandler, Edgar S. Washburn, William H. Latham, George F. Taylor, Arthur G. Turner.

Decoration,—George H. Purinton, Thomas Ashton, Hugh C. Murray, Everett H. Moulton, E. Clinton Winchester, James A. McAvoy, John Bowman, Marshall Tilden, John C. Lincoln, Albert S. Turner, John G. Keigwin, Joseph E. Monast, Charles E. Carpenter, Amos T. Fowler.

Printing and Advertising.—John A. McDonald, Arthur I. Bill, Allen B. Lincoln, William J. Sweeney, Charles R. Utley.

Programme.—John M. Hall, Edward F. Casey, Homer E. Remington, John L. Walden, M. Eugene Lincoln.

Memorial.—George W. Burnham, David C. Card, Frederick Rogers, John H. Moulton, Charles A. Capen, William H. Osborn, Frank H. Blish, John F. Carey.

Evening Entertainment.—Walter D. Brigham, Dennis F. Broderick, Jerome B. Baldwin, Adelard D. David, Huber Clark.

Fireworks and Amusement.—James H. Ross, Daniel P. Dunn, George H. Backus, Henry L. Edgarton, William N. Potter.

Music.—James E. Murray, Noah D. Webster, Charles B. Jordan, William C. Jillson, H. Clinton Lathrop.

Collation.—Joel W. Webb, Charles L. Boss, Luke Flynn, S. Chauncey Hooker, J. Octave Blanchette, William C. Backus, Charles Larrabee, Jr., Lester M. Hartson, Samuel E. Amidon.

Military Parade.—Lloyd E. Baldwin, John H. Morrison, Herbert R. Chappell, Patrick Fitzpatrick, Charles J. Fox.

Fireman's Parade.—Charles E. Leonard, James Tighe, Fred S. Young, John J. Henry, James E. Hanlon, John T. Bradshaw.

Citizen's Parade.—Charles B. Pomeroy, James E. Haggerty, George E. Stiles, George K. Nason, Moses Belair.

The original purpose in all these preparations was to hold the celebration in Willimantic, on May 12th, 1892, the bi-centennial anniversary of the incorporation of the town; the exercises to consist of historical addresses, exhibition of relics, etc., in the forenoon; a grand military and civic parade, with the local military, firemen, and fraternal bodies in line, also an industrial pageant of local industries, the Putnam Phalanx of Hartford, the Third Regiment, C. N. G., the Governor's Foot Guards of Hartford, and perhaps other outside organizations, all to make an imposing demonstration ; and to wind up with a grand banquet or entertainment with fireworks in the evening.

The town was asked to appropriate $2500 for expenses, and it was proposed to raise from $1500 to $2000 more by private subscription. But the town could not legally appropriate any sum for such a purpose without legislative authority, and the famous legislative "deadlock" of 1891-'93 was existing ; so it became necessary for private citizens to assure the $2500 desired from the town until the Legislature should in the future authorize the town to make the appropriation. The sum of $2500 was voted by the town, March 3rd, 1892, with proviso that it would be paid to the bi-centennial committee when the Legislature should validate it. On this basis James Walden patriotically set out to secure the $2500 guaranteed from 100 citizens who should pledge $25 each. He secured 67 of the necessary 100 without much difficulty, but it was seen that this plan would hinder the raising by private subscription of funds thought to be needed over and above the $2500 guarantee required to protect the town's appropriation. It now began to appear that there was considerable difference of opinion among citizens as to the historic appropriateness of the kind of celebration proposed. The citizens of Windham Centre, and with them not a few residents of Willimantic, felt that Old Windham Green, which had been the center of the town's inception and growth, and the scene of its chief activities for nearly 150 of the 200 years of its incorporate life, should be made more prominent in the celebration ; and many thought, indeed, that the celebration should be held there. Judge John M. Hall meanwhile suggested that rather than expend so much money for a parade, it were better to donate it towards a Memorial town building, which should at once meet the town's present needs and celebrate the bi-centennial event in a worthy and enduring manner. At a town meeting held March 26th, 1892, the permanent committee reported that "we find very little public enthusiasm on the subject" of the proposed celebration and "we refer the matter back to the town for further instructions." The town meeting therefore "*Voted*, that the whole matter relating to the bi-centennial celebration be abandoned." But John M. Hall, C. A. Capen, E. H. Holmes, C. E. Carpenter and J. O'Sullivan were appointed a committee to examine sites and present estimates and cost of a suitable Memorial building. At another meeting held April 30, the committee reported that they had examined various available sites. No definite action was taken but the committee was continued with instructions to examine further into the subject and report at such future time as seemed expedient. No further report has been had to date.

Many were disappointed that the plans for celebrating the bi-centennial celebration were abandoned. The residents of Old Windham Green promptly resolved that there should be a celebration, and one of a character suited to the occasion. They therefore went to work with enthusiasm and energy, and on Friday evening, March 31, a meeting was held in School Hall, at Windham Center, to perfect organization for the event.

The following officers were elected: President, Guilford Smith; vice-president, Henry Larrabee; secretary and treasurer, Frank F. Webb; general committee, Guilford Smith, Henry Larrabee, Frank F. Webb, Charles Larrabee, Jr., George Lathrop, George Challenger, E. H. Holmes, James G. Martin, H. C. Lathrop.

Honorary Vice-Presidents—Elisha Hammond, Thomas Ramsdell, John Perkins, Marvin Burnham, Andrew Frink, William Wales, Waldo Bingham, Rufus Rood, Henry Page, Charles Larrabee, Jairus Smith, Albert Perry, Rufus Huntington, Charles Smith, Jonathan Hatch, Freeman D. Spencer, Henry Spafford, Albert Hartson, L. E. Baldwin, John Brown, Harry Boss, George W. Burnham,

A. D. Loring, H. H. Fitch, F. M. Lincoln, J. C. Bassett, Lorin Lincoln, Chester Tilden, E. E. Burnham and Israel Robinson.

Special committees on finance, programme, decorations, relics and reception were appointed as follows :

Reception Committee—J. G. Martin, Wm. Swift, A. S. Winchester, E. P. Kenyon, Mrs. Ann H. Johnson, Mrs. Mary D. Taintor, Miss Mary Perkins and Miss Bertie Campbell.

Decoration Committee—L. J. Hammond, F. K. Hoyt, L. G. Frink, Wm. Larrabee, Wm. P. Barstow, Robert Stanton, Chester Woodworth, Miss Josie Bingham, Mrs. Julia Arnold, E. S. Yergason, Miss Mary Perkins, Mrs. Henry Hatch and Mrs. Chester Jewett.

Financial Committee—Harlow Holmes, Henry Hatch, Chester Jewett, Lester Hartson and Miss Emma Kenyon.

Programme Committee—H. C. Lathrop, Dr. F. E. Guild, T. J. Kelley, G. H. Alford and Mrs. F. F. Webb.

Collation Committee—Charles Larrabee, Jr., George Challenger, G. B. Peabody, C. H. Wilson, Arthur Williams, Mrs. Guilford Smith, Mrs. Henry Larrabee, Mrs. Eliza Loomis and Mrs. G. B. Peabody.

Relic Committee—George Lathrop, Horatio N. Bill, Prentiss Lewis, Miss Julia Swift, Miss Emma Larrabee, Mrs. Chas. Baker, Everett H. Moulton, DeWitt Lockman and Mrs. Sarah Holmes.

Town Committees—*Chaplin:* John Griggs, Edgar S. Lincoln, Origen Bennett; *Hampton*: David Greenslit, Henry Burnham, Geo. M. Holt; *Mansfield:* Dr. E. G. Sumner, I. P. Fenton, Prof. L. P. Chamberlain; *Scotland:* Wm. F. Palmer, Amos S. Chapman, C. M. Smith.

Thomas Snell Weaver, editor of the Willimantic Journal, was appointed historian for the first century ; Allen B. Lincoln of the New England Home, for the second century. It was planned to have an outdoor celebration on the old training ground, Windham Green, Wednesday, June 8, as there was not time to complete preparations by

May 12. It was announced that citizens from all sections of the town, and from those towns which were offshoots from the original settlement, were invited to unite in the ceremonies of the day.

THE CATHOLIC CELEBRATION.

While these preparations were going forward, another event occurred which should be recorded in this Memorial volume. It had been the intention of the Rev. Florimond De Bruycker of the local St. Joseph's Roman Catholic parish to signalize the bi-centennial celebration as at first proposed in Willimantic by unfurling on that day the American flag over the St. Joseph's parochial school. When the Willimantic celebration was abandoned, Father De Bruycker at once determined to change the flag-raising incident into a formal recognition of the bi-centennial date. Accordingly the bi-centennial was celebrated under Catholic auspices on Saturday, May 14, and the Willimantic Journal of May 20, gave the following account of it:

Saturday afternoon was made patriotic and eloquent by the Catholic citizens of Willimantic. Shortly after 2 o'clock a procession under escort of our local Co. E, Third Regiment, C. N. G., Capt. Robinson, made a half hour's parade through Main street, attracting a great number of sightseers. The Montgomery Hose Company, St. Jean De Baptiste Society, Ancient Order of Hibernians and Knights of Columbus, all local organizations, were in line and made a creditable showing. When the yard of St. Joseph's Parochial school was reached the procession filed in and with the thousand or more citizens already there made up a fine audience for the speakers to address. The buildings were trimmed with the national colors and on the north section of the broad verandah were ranged the children of the school who sang patriotic airs in the interim of the speakers and sang them well, their fresh, clear voices ringing out with a true, patriotic ring.

The exercises were conducted by Rev. Fr. De Bruycker, who gave a brief address of welcome and expressed the hope that all present would, by the celebration of the bicentennary of the town of Windham in this manner come to a better understanding of each other. The children present would be impressed by the occasion with a love for the flag and for the country and gain a sense of the great responsibilities which would rest upon them as they grew into citizenship. The flag was then unfurled by Thomas Ashton, a veteran Union soldier, and as it floated gracefully to the breeze a shower of red, white and blue stars fell from its folds. It was greeted with cheers and the song "Columbia, the Gem of the Ocean" by the school children. Father De Bruycker then very pleasantly introduced Commander B. E. Smith of the Grand Army of Connecticut and a resident of Willimantic, as one who knew what it was to maintain the flag. Commander Smith spoke of the sentiment of patriotism which gathered them in the place and said that there was no higher motive than that of loyalty to one's country and flag, and spoke of the knowledge the Union veterans had of the depth of that sentiment which impelled men to lay down their lives for its honor.

Dr. A. D. David then addressed the French-American citizens in the audience in their own own language. He told his fellow countrymen that while they need not for a moment forget the country of their nativity, yet they should love the country of their adoption with an affection that comes to the patriotic heart from a love of all that is noble and enduring. He spoke of the greatest and best loved of all Frenchmen in America, Lafayette, and closed with an impassioned appeal for the maintenance of the freedom he helped to establish here.

Principal A. B. Morrill of the Normal school, spoke of the peculiarity of the gathering as one indigenous to this country. Men of all beliefs and nationalities meet here for a common purpose and on common ground. This republic was not the first of the great republics of the world, but it differed from all the republics which have passed away in the fact that it conserved the welfare of all the people. So long as that principle was guarded, the republic would be safe and there would be a patriotic acquiescence in the will of the majority.

James T. Lynch referred to the settlement of Old Windham two hundred years ago and to the fact that her sons had taken part in all four of the wars which had occurred in the country, and besides had the battle of the frogs to care for. He was proud of the history of the grand old town and if there should ever be another war in which the honor of the country should be at stake there would be no Methodists, Baptists, Congregationalists, or Catholics, none but American citizens, possessed with one purpose and sentiment.

Rev. Fr. J. J. Quinn of Collinsville made an eloquent address in which he traced the influence of the Catholic church in the struggle for the republic, and paid a glowing tribute to Charles Carroll of Carrollton, a signer of the Declaration of Independence, who staked more upon the issue than any other signer, as he was the wealthiest of them all. Here in this republic there was no aristocracy, but that of brains, honesty and ability ; the republic would stand if we added patriotism, religion.

Gen. Thomas McManus of Hartford made a pleasant and humorous address and after thanks had been returned to the audience for its attention and presence, by Rev. Fr. De Bruycker, three cheers were given for the flag and the celebration was over.

ON WINDHAM GREEN.

The celebration on Windham Green occurred as planned, on Wednesday, June 8, 1892. It was thoroughly "Windhamese" in all respects, every feature of the programme having significance as to Windham and the towns that have sprung from her, and all the speakers being of Windham birth or connections. The Willimantic Journal of May 10, made substantially the following report of the proceedings:—

A modest and altogether appropriate celebration of the two hundredth anniversary of the incorporation of the town of Windham, was that held on Windham Green, Wednesday, the entire day being passed in the study of the grand history of the town from its earliest, down through colonial, revolutionary and the later times. To begin with the citizens of the Green had made their dwellings and surroundings brilliant with the stars and stripes, while the skies were dimmed just the slightest to shield the sun's glare, and the trees in their early leaf of tender green, swayed as if in kindly benison upon the gathering. In every direction from the tastefully decorated speakers' stand, [which was erected on the Green, almost directly across the road from the church parlors] historical landmarks, appropriately recognized, and the beautiful arrangements of bunting, pleased the eye. Prominent among the decorations were those upon and about the Colonel Dyer mansion, where General Washington stopped on his visit to the town. Bunting was tastefully displayed, a goddess of liberty stood upon the lawn, while a huge frog stood a non-croaking sentinel at the gateway. The house is now the property of L. J. Hammond, and here the speakers and distinguished guests were received and entertained by Mrs. Ann Johnson, as hostess, and Arthur S. Winchester as chairman of the reception committee. It was a beautiful spot wherein to pass an hour, conjuring up visions of what had passed beneath its roof in the trying days of those grand men who had so much to do with carrying forward the revolutionary war in New England. Near by was the Colonel Elderkin mansion, fittingly draped by its present occupant, William Swift, while down the Nipmuck path, the Joshua Elderkin house, the old Webb place, the Abbe house and others were hung with bunting. The old tavern, now kept by George Challenger, was properly decorated and the residences of John Perkins and Charlotte Lathrop, Willard Beckwith, Chauncey Wilson, Rufus Rood, Dr. Smith, and others were tastefully trimmed. At the Willimantic entrance to the Green was flung a beautiful arch of red, white and blue, with the legends "May, 1692—Welcome—May, 1892." Up on a branch of an elm tree in front of the old Staniford tavern, sat the little fat image of Bacchus, as nearly as could be in the location where he sat for so many years, until the old tree blew down, and that insatiable relic hunter, A. E. Brooks, captured him. Mr. Brooks gave the little fellow a car ride from Hartford on the early train that he might once again feast his eyes on familiar Windham Green. Down in the old cemetery John Cates, the first settler, slept beneath the stars and stripes, and if he was a fugitive, because of offenses to the crown of England, his spirit must have looked down with kindness upon the emblem which restless men, like he, had, years after his death, placed as an insignia of religious and political freedom.

At sunrise the booming of cannon and the ringing of the churchbells announced the opening of the day, and shortly after 8 o'clock the Nathan Hale drum corps of Coventry, with their continental uniforms, woke the echoes of the Green as they have not been since the regimental training days of General Baldwin. Hopkins and Allen's band of Norwich was soon in tune, with Charley Hatch of Hartford as leader, a Windham boy showing his Windham friends what good out-of-door music should be. Shortly after 10 o'clock the band led the procession of speakers and guests from the Colonel Dyer mansion to the speaking stand, where after a brief concert by the band, Guilford Smith, chairman of the day, rapped to order, and the exercises began. Rev. S. J.

Horton, D. D., of Cheshire, formerly of Windham, read a brief selection from an old version of the Scripture, printed in 1589, before the King James translation, which had been preserved by the Devotion family and is now the property of Mrs. Lee Lathrop of this city. Following are the passages which he read from Hebrews i., 10, 11, 12, xiii., 1. 2.

And, Thou, Lord, in the beginning haft laid the foundation of the earth; and the heavens are the works of thine hands.

They fhall perifh, but thou remaineft; and they all fhall wax old as doth a garment:

And as a vefture fhalt thou fold them up and they fhall be changed; but thy years fhall not fail.

Let brotherly love continue.

Be not forgetful to entertain ftrangers : for thereby fome have entertained angels unawares.

Mr. Horton then offered an appropriate prayer, after which Chairman Smith made a cordial address of welcome to the sons of old Windham, who had gathered for this celebration, and to the friends from other towns, who had come to look upon and gather lessons from the day. He then introduced Thomas Snell Weaver, and paid a compliment to his father, the late William L. Weaver, to whom the town owed so much for its knowledge of the past. Mr. Weaver reviewed the principal events of the first century of the town's history. A short selection by the band followed Mr. Weaver's paper, after which a poem, "At Home," composed by Miss Josephine M. Robbins of Chaplin, was read by Miss Nellie M. Griggs of Chaplin.

Hon. Edward S. Cleveland of Hartford, senator from the first Connecticut district, a native of Hampton, and of good Windham stock, made a characteristic address. He felt most highly complimented in being invited to be present and whatever inspiration he had for what he might say had been gathered from contemplation of the events outlined in the historical address to which he had listened. He paid tribute to the patriotism of the town that had been so full of heroic spirit, that had helped to maintain the rights of the people and uphold the flag in all the wars. He closed with an eloquent apostrophe to the nation's flag—"And now let us with town, state and national pride, praise with songs of pride our ancestors who guarded that flag from the foeman's steel."

Led by the band the audience joined in "America" and an hour's recess was had for dinner and a social gathering. There was abundant preparation for feeding the 2,000 or more people who were present. The speakers and guests were entertained in the chapel of the Congregational church, where the ladies served a banquet that would have done honor to the king of all caterers, whoever he may be. Grace was said by Rev. George Stearns, son of a former pastor of the Congregational church of Windham. During the intermission there were a great many hand shakings, cordial greetings and meetings of friends long since separated. It was a profitable hour for renewing acquaintanceships and for brief expressions of pride in the record of Old Windham.

The afternoon services began with the reading of a review of the history of the second century of Windham, by Allen Bennett Lincoln, editor of The New England Home of Hartford, and son of the late Allen Lincoln.

Then followed a poem appropriate to the occasion, written and delivered by the Rev. Theron Brown of the editorial staff of The Youths' Companion, a son of John A. Brown of Mt. Hope, and who was born in Willimantic.

At the close of Mr. Brown's poem, Edwin B. Gager, son of Lewis Gager of Scotland, but now of Birmingham, and judge of the Derby town court, spoke on behalf of Scotland.

Amos L. Hatheway, Esq., of Boston, son of A. Morris Hatheway, and maternal grandson of the Rev. Cornelius B. Everest, pastor of the Windham Congregational church in 1815-27, spoke of the significance of the life and character of the old New England town.

Charles Smith Abbe of Boston, a son of Windham and an actor in the Boston Museum company, gave a most felicitous bit of humor in an imaginary walk and conversation with John Cates, the first settler, in which were conjured up many merry things which kept the audience in splendid humor. It was a delightfully conceived fantasy, quaint, original and very funny, making a jovial ending to a day in which the eloquence of fact and eloquence of sentiment had vied with each other for the glory of two hundred years old Windham.

The historical addresses of Messrs. Weaver and Lincoln, the poems of Miss Robbins and the Rev. Mr. Brown, and the addresses of Messrs. Gager, Hatheway and Abbe, are given in full in the following pages. There is also printed in full the poem of Miss Jane Gay Fuller of Scotland, which was written for the occasion but by some misunderstanding did not reach the committee's hands in time to be read at the celebration. The Journal thus summarized the impromptu addresses of the other speakers of the day:—

Rowland Swift president of the American National bank of Hartford and a native of "Ponde Towne," spoke briefly of the close relationships which were found in the old colonial times, and told the story of the Windham girl who held the candle while her father shod the horses of Luzan's cavalrymen in the Revolutionary war, and to whom was presented the little flag of tri-color which was buried with her more than four score years after.

Dr. George Austin Bowen of Woodstock, master of the Connecticut State Grange, spoke of the agricultural interests which were the pride of the town of Windham, and of the great force and power the early farming community had.

The Old Windham Bank Building, with the legend "site of the Windham County Court House" over the doorway, and with another legend near by "site of the public whipping post," was converted into a museum of relics, to which many of the families of the town contributed largely. There were antique portraits, books, newspapers, "samplers" and a thousand and one things that space does not allow of chronicling here. It was visited all day long by crowds, many times it being almost impossible to move about, because of the number of interested persons examining the many curious and historical articles of value. Further reference to the relics exhibited will be found elsewhere.

There were many invited guests, mainly those who were from Windham originally, or were interested in historical matters. Among them were Miss Ellen F. Larned, author of the History of Windham County, Jonathan Flint Morris of Hartford, treasurer of the Connecticut Historical Society, Rowland Swift, E. S. Cleveland, P. H. Woodward, J. G. Rathbun, Chester Burnham, John M. Ney, Hart Talcott, Andrew F. Gates, Ward W. Jacobs, Nathan

Starkweather and many others from Hartford; Henry Allen, Hon. and Mrs. Lucius Brown, Reuben S. Bartlett, S. T. Holbrook, Wm. C. Lamnon, Arthur B. Webb, James P. Lathrop and others from Norwich; Mr. and Mrs. H C. Starkweather of New York, granddaughter of Zephaniah Swift of the Windham county court and minister to France; Mrs. E. H. Williams, widow of Judge Williams of Grand Meadow, Ia., Mrs. Emeline L. Perkins wife of Judge George Perkins of Fond du Lac, Wis., both sisters of Henry and Charles Larrabee of Windham; J. R. Cogswell of Putnam, a son of Windham; Rev. Horace Winslow of Simsbury a former pastor of the Willimantic Congregational church.

WINDHAM'S FIRST CENTURY.

BY THOMAS SNELL WEAVER.

Mr. President, Ladies and Gentlemen :

In briefly sketching the progress of Old Windham during the First Century of its existence, it will be necessary to go very lightly over the surface of events, otherwise your patience would be wearied, so full of rich detail were those eventful hundred years. There can but be, however, in a gathering like this for the express purpose of studying history, more than a passing interest in the general movement of the past, as it affects a locality full of tradition and deep interest, like the one where we are now met. Before entering upon the work, however, a single personal allusion will be pardoned. To the indefatigable research of my honored father, the late William L. Weaver, carried on under discouragements of an invalid life, with all matter at arms length from his table, and painstakingly and carefully pursued for more than six consecutive years, I am indebted for the greater amount of the data which will be used. I but feebly represent his undaunted historical spirit, his energy and his love for Old Windham, the town of his birth.

To begin at once then, Joshua Attawanhood, son of Uncas, the great Redskin of Eastern Connecticut, being sick in body but able and of disposing mind, February 29, 1675, by will granted to sixteen Norwich gentlemen of whom John Mason was chief, a tract about eight miles square, the northeastern boundary of which was at Appaquogue Pond near the northeastern corner of the now town of Hampton, and disposed to the westward and southward to the Willimantic and Shetucket rivers. He died while his father, the greater chieftain was yet living, and the proprietors of the tract came into possession of their grant May 27, 1676. The Nipmuck Indians, not a very powerful branch of the Mohegans, occupied the land in sparse numbers, probably coming to the rivers in the spring when the fishing was good, for they had some of the latter day instincts, and some of them remaining to plant and raise corn in the opens which were near the rivers. The greater portion of the tract was wooded and the path which the Nipmucks travelled in their journeyings to and from Uncas's headquarters near Norwich is now your Main street, according to the best tradition. No steps were taken to open up the tract to settlement immediately, as King Philip was making a great deal of trouble across the northern border and there was a continual movement of Indians over the tract for some years until that plucky redskin was fully cared for. Even then there was reluctance about settling here because of the possible trouble over Indian titles, which had been boldly disputed by Sir Edmund Andross, the colonial governor, who regarded them as no better than the scratch of a bear's paw. Andross, however, had his opinions very much modified by one Wadsworth. He was the man who thought to steal the charter of Connecticut colony. He changed his mind on that also.

The sixteen Norwich gentlemen were Captain John Mason, Daniel Mason and Samuel Mason, sons of Major John Mason, the famous Indian fighter, whose expedition against the Pequots was the most noted of all the events in the history of early eastern Connecticut, and who afterwards settled Norwich; Rev. James Fitch, Major James Fitch his son, John Birchard, Lieut. Thomas Tracy, Thomas Adgate, Simon Huntington, Lieut. Thomas Leffingwell, John Olmsted, physician, William Hyde,

William Backus, Hugh Calkins, Captain George Denison and Daniel Wetherwell. None of these settled in this town. They were mainly elderly men, who had been pioneers in the settlement of Norwich, and left for their sons and immediate descendants the work of building up this plantation.

An agreement to settle was made February 17, 1682, and each man signed, promising to content himself with the place where God's providence should determine by lot, to fix his particular tract of land,—a trustful faith in such matters quite in distinction from modern estate transactions. It was also agreed that only such wholesome inhabitants as the company shall see fit to admit shall purchase, so that the town in its beginning was select and aristocratic to a degree, and not a little of that flavor is said to exist even now.

John Mason had died and his brother Samuel had disposed of his interest, and John Post had purchased the right of John Olmsted, so that only fourteen proprietors signed this agreement, thirteen only of whom were grantees under the will of Attawanhood. These gentlemen, however, were all well-known pioneers in Eastern Connecticut filled with the spirit of breaking open the new country, with perhaps a little vein of speculation running through that. At all events when the settlement was actually made, those enterprising real estate dealers, the Masons and Fitches, had more than half the 60,000 acres of the tract in their possession, and there is a record to show that they sold even to the sons of those of whom they had bought. To offset this, however, they had the charge of Abimelech Sachem, for one third of his keep, his father's generosity in land to the whites having made him a pauper, a veritable "Lo, the poor Indian."

The survey of the lots was made by Lieutenant Thomas Leffingwell, Sergeant Richard Bushnell and Simon Huntington and the tradition is that they made their first night's camp east of the Natchaug river just below the Horse Shoe Bend, about opposite what is now the Willimantic Fair grounds. Whether this be true or not, tradition picked out a most lovely and beautiful clearing for these pioneers to sleep in beneath the May sky of 1685.

The lots were laid out in three sections, one at Hither Place, one at Willimantuck and one at the Pondes, or what is now Mansfield Center. The first occupant of the lands was John Cates, an individual about whom there has been some mystery, more than has ever been satisfactorily explained. He came in 1689 and with his negro, Joe Ginne, erected a rude shelter which was afterwards converted into a dwelling with the assistance of Jonathan Ginnings, who was the first white man with a family in the town and to whom the first white child was born. Whatever Cates might have been before he came to Windham, he was a respectable citizen here, took some part, though never officially, in town affairs and was well thought of. His will gave some portion of his estate to the church and the town and his memory might well remain undisturbed by any futile attempts to discover whether he was a regicide, as some suggest, or merely an adventurer, who for personal reasons did not care to have his affairs in England known. After Cates, the settlers came in rapidly and in 1691 the inhabitants petitioned the General Court for a town grant, Joshua Ripley, John Cates, Jonathan Crane, Joseph Huntington, William Backus, Jeremiah Ripley, Jonathan Ginnings, Richard Hendee, John Backus and John Larabee being signers to the petition. The names have been familiar to the inhabitants of the town to this day. These petitioners were all residents of the Center.

Ponde Towne or Mansfield was settled almost contemporaneously with the Center, and for a few years the two sections lived together comfortably and with religious peace, but trouble over the church-going and ministerial privileges arose and in 1701 Mansfield went her own way as a separate town. The details of the steps that resulted in this division have been recently published and there is no time to go over them here. The incorporation of the town of Windham was May 12, 1692, and the first town meeting was held here June 11 of the same year, two hundred years from Saturday of this week.

At that meeting provision was made for the support of the gospel, and Mr. Samuel Whiting, son of Rev. John Whiting, pastor of the First church in Hartford, was chosen pastor and served the people in the capacity of spiritual and general advisor until his death in 1725, thirty-three years after. He was a man of uncommon fervor in the pulpit, who mingled greatly with the people in their everyday transactions and who had large interests in real estate, his name appearing with great frequency in the early transfers of property in the town. His wife was Elizabeth Adams, whose mother Alice Bradford, granddaughter of Governor Bradford of the Mayflower, and her children, transmitted a goodly strain of Mayflower blood to many descendants of Windham families. Her oldest daughter married Joseph Fitch and Colonel Eleazer Fitch was their son, the handsomest man in the American army, who served at the head of the Fourth Connecticut troops in the French and Indian war and whose sense of honor, having been once a soldier of the king, did not allow him to take a prominent part in the revolution. Elizabeth Whiting married William Gager. William Whiting, a son, was Lieutenant Colonel at the siege of Louisburg, and at Lake George under Sir William Johnson. John Whiting was a colonel in the French and Indian war, and Mary, the ninth child, married Rev. Thomas Clap who succeeded her father in the Windham pulpit and was afterwards president of Yale college. Samuel, the twelfth child, was also a colonel in the French and Indian war and the thirteenth child, a daughter, married into the Salstonstall family, and a grandaughter was the wife of General Wooster of New Haven, a revolutionary soldier whose descendants were prominent in that town for years. The family of Samuel Whiting was one of the religious militant families of the early town. Its members could pray or fight as occasion demanded and whatever they did they did well. No family of eastern Connecticut

put better blood into its descendants nor allowed itself to
commingle with any better blood. It was very blue, but it
was tinged with the red blood of courage which sent the
Mayflower across the sea.

Rev. Thomas Clap was 23 years of age when he took
charge of the church here, but he impressed himself upon
the community by his scholarly accomplishments, his force
of character and his indomitable will. He ruled with a rod
of iron and his people endured it, although it was remarked
that when in 1739 he accepted the presidency of Yale college they acted like boys let out of school. The educational
influence of Mr. Clap, however, is not to be underrated.
He inspired a love for study in young men, as the list
of graduates of Yale college from Windham bear evident
witness. Benjamin and William Throop, both preachers,
Nathaniel, Enoch, Joseph, and Jabez Huntington, Joshua,
Vine and John Elderkin, Daniel Welsh, the noted preacher of Mansfield, Ebenezer Dyer, Perez, John, James and
Elijah Fitch, Asa Spaulding, Samuel Cary, Ephraim
Starkweather, Ebenezer Devotion, son of the Scotland
preacher, John Ellery, Zephaniah Leonard, Dyer Throop,
Hezekiah Bissell, Colonel Ebenezer Gray, Hezekiah Ripley, Bela Elderkin, all graduated from Yale before the revolution and all were more or less connected with the activities of the town.

Before leaving the religious movement of this early
part of the history of the town, a word for Rev.
Stephen White, whose term in the pastorate was over
fifty years, and whose influence was of great benefit to the
town. He was not of so aggressive a temperament as either
of his predecessors, but he was a preacher of conscientious
painstaking and a man of mild and sweet temper. The
closing years of his term were beclouded with ill health
and by a great deal of uneasiness in the parish, the influx
of worldliness which had come in with the largely-increased
population giving him a great deal of anxiety. His plaint
in his half-century sermon has a very modern sound, when
he speaks of profane swearing, disregard of the Sabbath,

unrighteousness and intemperance, which had no place when his pastorate began. He passed away in a discouraged state of mind, but the town itself was marvellously prosperous at the time.

Another remarkable man in the religious life of the town was Rev. Ebenezer Devotion, who was the first pastor of the church in Scotland parish. He was a man of great force and unexampled dignity, and while he took great delight in being a farmer and working with his own hands and his own strength, which was marvelous, week days, and was on common terms with his people, on Sundays it is said of him that he entered the church between two files of the worshippers who took off their hats that he might receive the respect due him. His service was from 1735 to 1771 and his work was for the great good of that section of the town. He served also in the general assembly and was an active force in all intellectual effort. His epitaph is a lofty specimen of that older and better tribute of dignified English which we seldom see in latter-day cemeteries.

The religious movement of the century was disturbed by the Separatist agitation, which is of itself worthy of special study, but for which there is now no time. And Mr. Clap says of an attempt of Israel Fulsome and his wife that they called into their house an Episcopal teacher and held disorganizing meetings, which like the pleasures of sin, were only for a season.

These four men had so much to do with the early religious and social life of the town that it has seemed impossible to pass by without this allusion. Seldom, if ever, even in Connecticut, have four such noble men been given to a town in its first century, have served it so long and so faithfully. To them much of the influence the town had in public affairs can be directly traced.

The geographical lines of the original tract and of the subdivisions made during the first century are worth a passing notice. Our neighbor to the south, Lebanon, held a tract very near to the rivers which were the southern boundary of Windham, but not quite. There was a strip of no-man's land which was in dispute between the towns, and settlers having purchased it, it was decided by the General Court that they could be better accommodated if the tract was given to Windham to govern rather than to Lebanon. In this Lebanon readily acquiesced as she foresaw the bridging of the rivers. Windham, with a speculative eye thought of the fisheries and took the land for the shad, taking both the shad and the bridge while Lebanon had neither. She made a miss that time.

Mansfield was set off in 1701 and Hampton or Canada parish went its own way in 1786 after having for many years been a contributory parish of great value having maintained a church of its own; for since 1723 the parish was called Canada or "Kennedy" parish from David Canada or Kennedy its first settler. Isaac Magoon, the first settler in Scotland, gave the name to that parish as he was a Scotchman.

While the religious movement of the century was fraught with the greatest benefit to the educational and social life of the town, the secular and commercial side of the town was not neglected. Religious liberty was abundant, from the point of view of the colonists, and they soon branched out into those industries which became a part of the new settlement. The timber was cleared and saw mills were erected on Merrick's brook, the Shetucket and Willimantic rivers, and grist mills for the grinding of the grain raised on the plantation. The raising of cattle and sheep, carding and spinning wool and weaving it into the cloths necessary for the comfort of the settlers, all were carried forward with energy and the push consequent upon the condition of a rapidly growing community. While the earliest settlers came here from Norwich, and were descendants, many of them of the original proprietors, the bulk of the settlers coming in during the first half of the century were from the colonial towns on Massachusetts Bay. Salem, Rehoboth, Cambridge, Charlestown, Newton and other places contributed to the energy of the new population and the families were of a sterling and vigorous type.

The Abbes, Larabees, Cranes, Backuses, Durkees, Huntingtons, Flints, Snells, Jenningses, Allens, Binghams, Browns, Bibbinses, Badgers, Babcocks, Basses, Billingses, of whom the Hampton minister was a noble man and true, Carys, Elderkins, Fitches, Dyers, Clevelands, Clarks, Dingleys, Dimmocks, Denisons, Frinks, Follets, Grays, Hebards, Hunts, Kennedys, Kingsburys, Lincolns, Lathrops, Mannings, Martins, Murdocks, Millards, Moultons, Ormsbys, Palmers, Perkinses, Reeds, Ripleys, Robbinses, Robinsons, Rudds, Skiffs, Spaffords, Smiths, Spencers, Sawyers, Simonses, Stanifords, Southworths, Tracys, Taintors, Webbs, Waleses, Waldens, Warners, Woodwards, Welches, Whites, Whitings, Waldos, were all typical families, many of them having descendants in the town to-day, and many of them having furnished men of great distinction and of service to the state and to the country. In 1700 the first meeting-house was built on the home lot of William Backus which had been purchased for the purpose by Mr. Whiting and Ensign Jonathan Crane. This fixed the location of Windham Green where we are today, and during the century which followed it became historic ground. Here were all the public gatherings, the training days, here the courts were held after their establishment, and here the great men of the time stopped on their way from Hartford to Providence or Norwich. Many of the revolutionary heroes were here, and it is not at all unlikely that Washington often visited here when on his calls to Brother Jonathan Trumbull in Lebanon. There are many traditions as to this fact but no record that I am aware of.

Connecticut was unusually prosperous and the happiest of all the colonies in the early part of the century. There was freedom from Indian troubles, the colony was independent, and the conditions were right for peace and the pursuit of the industries which opened for the new settlements. The utility of the Sliding Fall at Willimantic was early seen and an iron works established there, the ore being dug in Mansfield. This industry was prosecuted with varying degrees of ill luck until, after its abandonment, it was swept away by a flood. But little attention was paid to that particular section of the town after this, until in the 'seventies, but the hay from the meadows was regularly housed by the farmers on the Green to help winter their stock, of which they had become large raisers. Benjamin Millard, who lived near the crotch of the rivers at the Horse Shoe bend, was allowed to set up a tannery in 1700, and Jonathan Crane was licensed by the General Court at Hartford to keep a victualling house for the entertainment of strangers and travellers and the retailing of strong drink. He was the first landlord of the first hotel and his license came, as will be seen, from headquarters. It was before the days of county commissioners. There was a rigid line of conduct in regard to common rights. The town granted and allowed what rights should be used on the rivers, and when Jonathan Bingham fenced in a spring for his own private use he was prosecuted and fined. Schools at the beginning were not much thought of, but Thomas Snell was allowed to keep one in his house, which was the first of the school privileges in town. In 1713 two schoolhouses were ordered; one to be set on the Green and one in the east of the town, Scotland. Highways received unusual attention and the town frequently called upon this or that delinquent to assist in keeping his share of the highway in good repair. Arrangements were also made with towns near by for the maintenance of sections of road which had become great public thoroughfares. In 1713 the meeting house, never a good one, was enlarged and a committee was appointed to seat the attendants upon worship according, first, to the place or station they are in, second, to the age they bear, and third, to the estate they enjoy. What became of those who had neither station nor estate is not quite clear.

The turning point in the great prosperity and success of Windham, was in the erection of Windham county and its selection as the shire town. This gave unwonted

stimulus to all kinds of activity and at once
made it the seat of public affairs, created a new
impetus in its life and really was the making of the
town. The necessity for concerted action on the
part of the towns was made manifest by the rival claimants to their county government. Woodstock was claimed
by Suffolk county, Massachusetts, Windham and Ashford by Windham and Hartford, and New London county
claimed the rest. The inconvenience was great, and
after an agitation lasting nearly eight years the county
was organized and Windham made the county seat. It
was the largest of the towns and really the most accessible, as the county contained towns to the west and south,
Coventry and Lebanon. Windham was not, however, at
the time, the wealthiest, Lebanon's ratable property being some £3,000 greater. The property in Windham was
largely in the hands of the few, the early comers having
the best of the land, while the mass of the people were in
hard straits. Money was scarce and the poorer people
could barely subsist on what they could raise. There
were no industries other than those of farming. The social condition at this time is known but little of, but the
religious state of the town was at its highest. There had
been a great revival under the ministrations of Mr. Whiting and the settlement had been thoroughly aroused.
There were a great many poor but pious parents, and the
families were large, frequently going into the 'teens in
numbers. The habitations were by no means grand, but
they were reasonably comfortable for first dwellings. The
first court held was that of common pleas, June 26, 1726,
Timothy Pierce of Plainfield, presiding, having been
raised from judge of probate to judge of the county court.
Joshua Ripley of Windham, Thomas Huntington of Mansfield, Joseph Adams of Canterbury, and Ebenezer West
of Lebanon, were justices of the quorum; Richard Abbe
of this town was treasurer of the county and Eleazer
Cary, Jonathan Crane, Joshua Ripley, jr., Joseph Huntington, Thomas Root and Nathaniel Rust were jurymen.

Forty-six cases were tried and from that time litigation was abundant. Jabez Huntington of Windham was the first sheriff. Mr. Abbe's back room in his dwelling was ordered to be a common jail until a new one should be built, which was very soon, however, and Mr. Abbe's back room was relegated to its original uses. In 1729 the county court house was planned and built in the succeeding year, the land being deeded by Thomas Snell, who at the time was a prosperous merchant. Soon after this Richard Abbe opened his mansion, by far the finest in town, as a place of public entertainment and for years it was the central point in the town. Business and trade centered, tanning was carried on by Nehemiah Ripley and Joseph Jennings. This state of prosperity continued until nearly the middle of the century, when there was a temporary check. Many of the prominent settlers and leading men died, there appeared no one to take their places, and there was an interim of dullness until after the close of the French war. Just previous to this, in 1740 and 1746, two young men, graduates of Yale College, were admitted to the bar and settled in Windham, their native town, and their public services in the great branches of public life, judicial and military, added lustre to the town. They were, by their long and distinguished services, until they died in the town, more than fifty years after, the most illustrious of the citizens: Colonel Eliphalet Dyer and Colonel Jedediah Elderkin. In 1745 the first execution in the county occurred in this town, that of Betty Shaw for the crime of infanticide. Roger Wolcott was chief judge, and the trial attracted great attention. The hanging was on Gallows Hill, and there was a great concourse on that coldest of cold days, December 18, 1745. Tradition has it that the hands and feet of the officers of the law were frozen, and that the victim's fingers rattled like icicles against the coffin upon which she sat on her way from the jail to the gallows. Alas, for poor, simple minded, much-sinned-against Betty Shaw. Those were days of wrath and not of sympathy. Her story is worthy the pen of a Hawthorne, but it rests a charge against the unforgiving spirit and severe judgments of our ancestors.

And now for the event which has made Windham known more than almost any other in its history, and which has afforded amusement and speculation ever since it is alleged to have happened, that great Batrachian Battle that occured on a murky night in 1754, about a mile east, at the frog pond. This has been celebrated in song and told of in story and just what the facts are no one exactly knows. There was undoubtedly some unusual disturbance among the frogs, and there was curiosity, if not alarm, on the part of the inhabitants. Peters, who for good reasons was not fond of Connecticut, says the frogs went in search of water to the Shetucket river, and that they filled a road forty rods wide, five miles long. Surely such an enfilading of frogs was ne'er writ about before, and if true it may be fair to presume that the frogs had heard that some of the settlers in Scotland were French Huguenots and ran away from their traditional enemies, the French. It is likely however that, the pond having been drawn off, the frogs suffered for water and made a large amount of noise about it before they died. There might have been a pitched battle and if so we shall have to accredit the frogs with assimilating the militant spirit of the settlers, who were in arms for the advance of the French and Indians, and fought it out in one night instead of taking all summer.

At all events the occurence has found its way into traditional literature, and Windham's descendants the world over are likely to be confronted with a bullfrog at almost any unexpected turn.

At the close of the French and Indian war there was a renewed wave of prosperity sweeping over the town. James Flint, Ebenezer Backus and Ebenezer Devotion, Jr. established an extensive trade, buying up the products of the town and exchanging them for West India goods. Wool growing, cattle raising, tobacco raising to some extent, and hemp culture were engaged in, and wheat was grown for exportation. The trade with West India stimulated all

STANIFORD TAVERN, WITH "BACCHUS" ON THE TREE.   WINDHAM GREEN ABOUT 1827.   FITCH TAVERN.

enterprises and saltpeter, leather, and even silk manufacture was begun, Jedediah Elderkin planting a mulberry orchard in South Windham and making a coarse silk which was used for handkerchiefs. In 1760 there were twelve places in the town where liquor was licensed to be sold, and Mercy Fitch of the Green kept one of them. In such a state of prosperity and accompanying cheer the life of the town was lively indeed, and the place was noted for the lavishness of its hospitality and for general jollity. Parson White's efforts in the pulpit to check this state of levity and worldiness were of little avail. Old Windham was hardened to a season of enjoyment. In 1760 the Susquehanna company, which had organized just before the outbreak of the French and Indian war for the purpose of taking up the land in the beautiful Wyoming valley, was reinvigorated, and Colonel Eliphalet Dyer went to England to get the approval of the crown of a purchase made of the Six Nations, the land in question being included in the charter of the state according to Connecticut belief. His mission was unsuccessful, but after a calling together of the company at Windham it was agreed to enter in and occupy, the King's command to the contrary. The state government had no desire to enter into any relations with the scheme as Pennsylvania also claimed the land. In '69 however some forty pioneers went to the valley and began the struggle for its possession. Of the forty, Captain John Durkee, Thomas Dyer, Vine Elderkin, Nathaniel Wales and Nathan Denison, were of Windham. No amicable agreement could be made with Pennsylvania although Colonel Dyer and Major Elderkin made an attempt at one. The Connecticut men, however, managed to keep their grip, and after reverses in which Fort Durkee was captured and lost and captured again, the settlement was made and the Windhamites held the ground, many emigrants going from their rocky surroundings to that most beautiful of the middle state valleys. All was prosperity there for a time until during the revolution in 1778 that base act of barbarity designed by the British, aided by the Indians, the

Wyoming massacre, occurred. The story of that foul blot on the conduct of the war with the colonies would be sufficient for a volume by itself. Women and children were murdered in their homes and the men in the fields, and when it was over the remnant made their way homeward to Connecticut, a party of a few hundred women and children with only one man to lead. The sufferings of that journey were participated in by the ancestors of some who are in this audience, without doubt. The Wyoming tract was afterwards added to Pennsylvania and Connecticut received the Ohio reservation from which the state school fund was largely made up. Thus Windham's enterprise fixed itself for good upon one of the institutions of which the state has long been proud. After the Revolution, there was again a tide of prosperity and at the close of it the first newspaper, "The Phoenix," or Windham "Herald," was founded, leaving a record behind of the transactions and life of the town.

The military spirit which pervaded the town has been purposely ignored in consideration, thus far, that it might make a fitting close to this incomplete review. Early in the century when there was danger of an Indian outbreak, a training company was organized. John Fitch was elected captain and Jonathan Crane lieutenant. From that time on there were regular training days and the usual development of colonels, majors, captains, etc. But show military display was not all that was to be had of old Windham. When the French and Indian war broke out a number of Windham men joined the regiment raised in eastern Connecticut to assist in the reduction of Crown Point under the command of Sir William Johnson. Eliphalet Dyer was lieutenant colonel, Captain Eleazer Fitch commanded one of its companies, raised almost entirely from Windham. Colonel Dyer was afterwards in command in the regiment with full rank. The services of Windham's soldiers in that war were notable, and many of them suffered the hardship of capture and torture by the Indians. Three of the sons of Minister Samuel Whiting, Nathan, Samuel and William, were colonels in that war, and Colonel Nathan Whiting and Colonel Eleazer Fitch were present at the surrender of Montreal to Lord Amherst.

At the first dawning of the revolution, the town of Windham enlisted in the cause of the country and thenceforward continued to serve it with energy and patriotic zeal. She was among the first to enter and the last to retire from the conflict. The blood of her sons was poured out on every battlefield of that great struggle from Bunker Hill to Yorktown. The passage of the stamp act in 1765 aroused an active resistance and the people of Windham were of those who determined that no stamps should be sold in the state; and some two hundred men from this and New London county mounted on horse back, proceeded to Hartford and Wethersfield, and compelled Jared Ingersoll, the stamp collector, to resign. Windham had a large contingent in that company and on its return from Hartford it halted for a night on Windham Green and enjoyed an evening of great hilarity, burning Ingersoll in effigy among other things. That was undoubtedly one of the liveliest nights ever seen on this spot of ground.

In 1768 a non-consumption ordinance was passed, and liberty meetings where the greatest enthusiasm was manifested were frequent. In June, 1774, a remarkable town meeting was held and a long and patriotic address was adopted. The appeal was this:

"Let us, dear fellow Americans, for a few years at least, abandon the narrow, contracted principle of self love which is a source of every vice; let our hearts expand, and dilate with the noble and generous sentiments of benevolence, though attended by the severer virtue of self denial. The blessings of heaven attending, America is saved. Children yet unborn will rise and call you blessed. The present generation will be extolled and celebrated to the latest period of American glory, as the happy instruments under God of delivering millions from thraldom and slavery, and securing permanent freedom and liberty to America."

And those old Windham men meant what they said. When the news of Lexington spread through the New England towns, Windham sent four companies of 150 men to Bunker Hill in Colonel Elderkin's regiment, and more followed. Some of these first recruits sleep at the foot of Bunker Hill monument in Charlestown, and, among the graves in Windham cemetery, there is one tombstone which reads, "The grave of Joel Webb, a soldier of the revolution who fought at Bunker Hill." He was 26 years of age when he left this Green for the scene of battle.

There are good reasons for believing that during the war more than 1,000 soldiers went from this town, and at one time there were 300 in the field. On one occasion Washington complimented a contingent from Windham as thoroughly reliable, and gave them a special commission of a hazardous nature. Time fails to give account of the officers and men and their heroic deeds. They fought and starved and took the hazard of fortune which came to those brave continental soldiers, and the world has seen no better stuff behind muskets.

Incidental to the war, Elderkin and Wales manufactured a good share of the powder used by the continental troops, at the mills in Willimantic, while Hezekiah Huntington, who had a major's commission in the army, remained at home, repairing and manufacturing arms at the old iron works in the same locality. The United States government early had this location in view as a proper site for the United States armory which was afterwards built in Springfield, Massachusetts; but the latter state had a stronger "pull" than Connecticut, or Willimantic would have made muskets and rifles to-day, instead of thread and cotton cloth, and silk. Eliphalet Dyer, Nathaniel Wales jr., and Joshua Elderkin were members of the committee of safety and doubtless often met with Jonathan Trumbull and Washington in the Lebanon war office.

The conspicuous Windham men of the century were:

First and foremost Samuel Huntington, signer of the

Declaration of Independence, for a brief time president of the Continental Congress, succeeding John Jay, and for ten years governor of Connecticut. He was also a chief justice of the superior court. He was a man of great ability, a devoted and sincere Christian who served his generation with judgment and faithfulness. He is one of the immortals whose signature to that old parchment of July 4, 1776, in Philadelphia, should give a tinge of pride to every true-born Windham son.

Colonel Eliphalet Dyer was a man of great energy, a member of the Continental Congress from 1774, and a military man of high ability. He was respected more than any man who spent his life in the town. He lived to the good age of 87 years and in all the various dignified stations he had occupied, both civil and military, he was distinguished for his highly useful talents and the faithful and honorable discharge of his important duties.

Rev. Eleazer Wheelock, D. D., who established the famous Indian charity school at Lebanon, was a native of Windham and his long march to New Hampshire to found Dartmouth college, is one of the educational facts of importance to New England.

Colonel Jedediah Elderkin, Colonel Ebenezer Gray, and others, there is no time to mention in detail.

I have thus briefly reviewed the principal movements of Windham, the religious, secular, commercial and military, during the first century of its history. Much has been omitted, much has but feebly been outlined. Enough, however, has been done to show to this, a later generation, that their ancestry and that of the town is something in which we may well have a patriotic pride. There have been lessons of self-denial, courage and persistence brought to our view. No one can look upon the history of that eventful century, as Windham, a typical colonial town, reveals it, without a feeling of warmth and reverence for those who founded and carried on its activities. How can we help loving old Windham? As a gifted son of the town has sung when once more he visited familiar scenes and climbed again the gray old hill :—-

Obwebetuck, once more with grateful feet,
   I tread at eventide thy mossy height,
Forget the city's crowd, the noisy street.
   And feast upon the landscape with delight.

Afar encircling hills shut in the view,
   Within, green fields and woods refresh the eye,
While just below Shetucket's line of blue,
   Reflects the glory of the parent sky.

I see the village, nestling as of old,
   Beneath the shade of sycamores and elms,
Its roofs and spires suffused with sunset gold.
   The past comes back and memory overwhelms.

A little nearer lies the grassy slope,
   Where sleep the early lost, but still endeared.
No marble mockery of faith and hope,
   No broken shaft above their dust is reared,

But simple tablets cut from native stone,
   Record the names of venerated sires,
And show the narrow path by which alone
   Our souls can satisfy their deep desires.

There dwell the living whom I fondly love,
   Here rest the weary whom I long to see,
And in the kindling heaven that bends above,
   Our blest abode, our Paradise shall be.

Dear Windham, if my wayward heart forget
   My mother's birthplace and her kindred's home,
With none to miss me, none to feel regret,
   May I be doomed through earth's wide waste to roam.

WINDHAM'S SECOND CENTURY.

BY ALLEN BENNETT. LINCOLN.

INTRODUCTORY.

Human thought has suggested but one Being to whom "an hundred years are as a day." For one of His creatures to attempt to comprehend a century of history in forty minutes is to attempt the impossible.

Liberal borrowing from published volumes, inquiry of old traditions, and prompt responses to my letters by many interested, have brought me a flood of information concerning Windham's second century, which I have had barely time to compile, but not to comprehend.

I shall be able to read but a few suggestive passages, which I hope may serve to indicate to you something of what the life and character of the town of Windham has been for the past 100 years.

TOPICS.

Old Windham, North and South Windham,
Early Willimantic, Willimantic Manufactures,
The Borough, Windham in Reforms,
The Old State Militia, Old Windham of To-day,
The Churches, Old Landmarks,
The Railroads, Willimantic's Newspapers,
The Schools, Notes of Interest,
Windham in War, Our Present Population,
The Future.

OLD WINDHAM.

The opening of the second century finds Old Windham in the zenith of her glory and in the beginnings of her decline.

An hundred years of growth had ripened her into the foremost inland town east of the Connecticut river. Norwich and New London surpassed her in wealth and numbers, because they were at tide water, but Windham surpassed even them in influential association with the head centers of government. The brilliant Samuel Huntington of Scotland Parish, ex-president of the Continental Congress and late chief justice for Connecticut, was now in the sixth year of his decade of service in the governor's chair, and he made frequent visits to his old home. Zephaniah Swift,* the young lawyer from Tolland county who had settled in Windham years before, and had become the oracle of local wisdom for many miles around, was chosen to congress in 1793, and this gave Windham direct association with the centers of national influence. Judge Swift was one of the most remarkable men of his time and was widely sought for his practical advice in affairs. His famous "Swift's Digest," compiled here in Windham after he left Congress, was long a standard among law books, and still ranks among the classics of the profession. The clergy, lawyers, doctors and business men of Windham were of high order of intelligence and took a lively interest in public affairs. The Windham "Herald," established in 1791, was fast gaining a wide circulation, reaching about 1,200 copies during its first decade, and it served to make Windham the center of actual information as well as of intellectual prestige.

---

* Judge Swift was a native of Old Plymouth county, but in early childhood came to Lebanon, and graduated at Yale in 1778, when fifteen years old ; studied law and settled for a brief time in Mansfield, then came to Windham. He was naturally adapted to public life and received rapid advancement. He entered the legislature in 1787, was speaker of the house in '92, went to congress in '93, and soon after was secretary of a legation to France. Later he was for eighteen years a superior court judge, and the five latter years chief justice His various legal writings brought order to the confusion of the common law. He was the moving spirit in the revision of the Connecticut Statutes in 1821. Here at Windham he wrought out that invaluable working manual "Swift's Digest." He lived in the spacious mansion on the crown of the hill east of the village now occupied by the family of the late George S. Moulton. Judge Swift died at the age of 64.

Mrs. Emily Lucretia Huntington Starkweather Grand-daughter - of Chief Justice Swift

Here, too, was the center of commercial activity. The old Green was a lively trading center. Here were several small manufactures, large and progressive for those days, and a score or more of stores, where the prosperous farmers of the vicinity bartered their products for the dry and wet goods brought from the New York market and the West Indies. Here stockings and mittens were made from home-grown wool, and large flocks of sheep dotted the hillsides. Col. Elderkin wove silk fabrics from his own mulberry orchard for his favored daughters and for the New York market. Elisha Abbe's stanch and dapper little craft, "The Windham," with a frog militant at her bow, plied the coast waters in the carrying trade as proudly as her more pretentious rivals. Here on the Green was "the largest drug store in Eastern Connecticut," wherein Col. Dyer's son Benjamin had kept his fabulous stock worth 1,000 pounds. Col. Dyer had built a dam across the Shetucket at South Windham, and another at the Frog Pond, and saw and grist mills were operated at these and other points. Henry DeWitt, a convict at the county jail, had caught the industrial inspiration and by deft handiwork wrought headed tacks out of old iron, and thus won rank among the pioneers in tack manufacture.

As shire town since 1726, Windham was also at this time the great center of all county gatherings, not only for courts and political conferences, but for religious associations as well, in which its "First Church" was a leader. Here too was Windham Academy, finishing school for her own thirteen populous districts, and educational center for surrounding towns. The population of Windham at this time, including Scotland and parts of Chaplin, Lebanon and Columbia, was somewhat over 2,500. Over at "Willimantic Falls" there was only a grist mill and a tannery, besides the disused powder mill and iron works, and nothing to foreshadow the future, save that old "Uncle" Amos Dodge had predicted that a great settlement would one day grow out of the privileges of the rapid water fall.

Such was Windham at the opening of the second century. But her glory was more ripened than growing, and decline had already set in.

The most potent factor of disintegration was religious dissension. The Separatist agitation was in its last stages. The demoralization and burdens of war had fanned the flame of dissatisfaction with the existing order. The men of the Dyer and Elderkin stamp, who had been so influential on orthodox and established lines, were passing away, the infidel influences of the French revolution, added to our own newly-acquired freedom from kingly rule, led to a relaxation in moral and civil affairs that was disastrous for a time, until the rising generation came to a clearer appreciation of the responsibilities, as well as the privileges, of civil and religious liberty. But this will appear in detail when we come to review the status of the churches. Suffice it to say that with the first decade of our new century, there comes a decline of public spirit and unity, a scattering of the forces that had made Old Windham what she was, and a looking towards new fields of development.

The first avenue which led people away from Old Windham was the upbuilding of the great Turnpike lines for through travel by stages. True, they brought to her hotels an increasing patronage and for a time made her more of a center of hospitality than ever, but they also opened the eyes of her young men to the outside world and her population continued steadily to decline. The Windham Turnpike Company was organized in 1799 to equip the road from Plainfield to Coventry, as a part of the through system from Hartford to Providence. Timothy Larrabee was the moving spirit in this enterprise and the next year he led in another company to build a turnpike from Franklin to Stafford, an extension of the New London & Norwich line, which afterwards went on to Springfield. The building of turnpikes led also to the general development of better roads to surrounding towns.

Four-wheeled wagons made their first appearance in

Windham in 1809 and were the wonder of the time, few believing that a horse could ever draw one. In 1818 the Natchaug river was bridged at what is still called the "Horseshoe" bridge (because of the shape in the bend of the river just above) and direct connection with Willimantic Falls was thus secured.

During the stage-coach days Windham's taverns became famous for their generous and free-hearted hospitality. The most famous was the Fitch tavern, which stood on the site of the present Windham hotel. Its distinctive sign, then the type of the times, was the "jolly rotund Bacchus," as the image was then called, which was perched aloft on the sign post, but which looks to the advancing intelligence of to-day more like a grinning, bloated idiot than an attractive type of pleasure. Later the old Stanniford Inn was in its glory, standing where Thomas Ramsdell's house now is, and with a magnificent elm, long since gone, spreading its hospitable branches over the inn and green. On an arm of that elm the Bacchus image rested for many years until, some time after the Washingtonian movement, a great gust of God's righteous breezes broke off the limb and the image descended. It is still preserved by A. E. Brooks of Hartford. There were a dozen or more smaller houses that entertained the numerous travellers who came this way. Henry Larrabee well remembers the four-horse coaches that passed here daily in 1840, from north, south, east and west. There were several smaller stage lines for mail service, from Windham to Woodstock, Middletown and other points. Such were the modes of public travel until the advent of railroads in 1849.

Windham took keen interest in the movement for the state constitution which culminated in 1818. The underlying motive of its advocates was to overthrow the church tax and leave men free to worship as they chose. The Federalist party, maintained on conservative lines, was falling to pieces. It was only by showing liberal tendencies that Judge Swift had been chosen to Congress. The

"Sectaries" entered then with increased vigor the movement for a new constitution. Peter Webb, a leading merchant and Republican (as the Democrats of those days were called) boldly declared that the Connecticut Charter was "no constitution at all" and to the consternation of the Conservatives there was sufficient approval of the sentiment to elect him to the legislature in 1804, and thereafter he and others of similar view were repeatedly sent up to the General Court. It is interesting to note that the same argument was made against constitutional reform that we hear so much in the present similiar movement, namely, that the instrument was "too sacred" to be disturbed and that disaster would follow the repeal of ancient customs. But the vigorous Windham reformers kept right on, and Peter Webb was one of three chosen from Windham county to help draft the constitution of 1818.

The decisive blow to Old Windham's prestige and the last great mark of her decline was the removal of the court house and county seat to Brooklyn in 1819. She had been shire town for nearly a hundred years, and all the interests of this section had centered here. But now, —disintegrating influences were at work all around her. The northern towns of the county had grown in population and influence and objected to travelling so far for public conveniences. To the west, young Willimantic was drawing away citizens and industries and opening up new fields. As early as 1797 Timothy Larrabee and others had met representatives of the northern towns to counteract their movement against Windham's shire-town privileges. The struggle was long and hotly contested. But in 1819 the General Court decreed that Brooklyn should have the coveted privilege, and Windham was reluctantly forced to yield. The county-seat question has ever since been one of intermittent interest, and even now lingers with suggestive possibilities. For years after the removal to Brooklyn, Windham fought to regain at least half-shire privileges, but to no avail. Chaplin, portions of

Columbia and Lebanon, which had made her their judicial center, now drew away, and Old Windham's day was over. But in later days these same towns have come to look upon the new Windham at Willimantic as their natural center in trade. The modern drift of people and business to large towns has left Brooklyn more completely at one side than ever Old Windham was left, and the partial shire privileges granted to Willimantic in recent years suggest that a new county of the towns surrounding her is not an impossible thing.

EARLY WILLIMANTIC.

With the loss of the county seat, attention centered at once upon the growing settlement at Willimantic as the hope of the town.

The years 1822-1827 were big with prophetic events. As early as 1806 a machine for picking and carding sheep's wool had been set up at "The Falls," in the mills of Clark & Gay, to supplement the saw, grist and paper mills. But Eli Whitney's great invention marked a new era of manufacture, and Willimantic, in common with all the valleys of Eastern Connecticut, was soon attacked with the cotton fever. The rapid fall of the river,—about ninety-one feet between the Windham Company's and the Shetucket Junction,—had given the place its early name and now proved a rare attraction to manufacturers.

First came from Providence in 1822 Perez O. Richmond, who with the financial aid of Solomon Loring, father of A. Dunbar Loring, built a little cotton spinning mill near the present site of the Linen Company's No. 3. Then came the Jillson Bros., William from Rhode Island, and Asa and Seth from Dorchester, Mass., and built three mills, one now remaining, (the present spool shop), also the old Duck mill and another three-story structure, both of which stood next east of the spool shop, but were later removed for the Linen Company's present structures.

The Jillsons built in 1824 the "old stone row" of tenement houses which used to stand along the north bank of the river about where the N. Y. & N. E. R. R.'s south spur track now runs. Tingley & Watson of Providence started the Windham Company's mill at its present location in 1823, building the main mill, and the new east mill was built in 1827. Deacon Charles Lee of Windham had meanwhile started a little mill on the site of the present Smithville Company's plant, and built the row of white tenement houses north of the mill on Main street, and in 1827 the stone store and boarding house, still standing at the corner of Bridge and Main streets. But Deacon Lee's enterprise never obtained a foothold, and not much was done at this site until the Smithville Company was organized in 1845, by Messrs. A. D. and J. Y. (afterwards Governor) Smith of Rhode Island, who put Whiting Hayden in charge and built up a prosperous industry.

The building of these mills in the early '20s was the one theme of conversation for years. Fabulous stories were told of the wealth of the men who could rear such stately structures! The employees of those days were of the native stock.

Interesting recollections of the polling places of the early part of the century have come to hand. After the county seat was removed, the voting was done in the church at Windham Centre until the Townhouse was built in 1835. Contention soon arose from Scotland on the one side and Willimantic on the other that it was not convenient to travel to Windham to vote. For a time, therefore, it was arranged that the voting should be done by turns, one year at Windham Green, the next at Scotland, the next at Willimantic, and so on. But of course this plan was still more unsatisfactory, especially for the extremes of Willimantic and Scotland, so the polling place was returned to Windham Center, and there remained until removed to Willimantic about 1862. The town records were removed about the same time, William Swift, son of Justin, and the leading merchant and citizen of later Windham Center and for many years town clerk, was succeeded by Allen Lincoln, one of the most active promoters of the rapid upbuilding of Willimantic after the war of '61-'5, and who remained town clerk 17 years. Scotland foresaw that Willimantic was destined to overshadow Windham Center, and not wishing to go so far for her public conveniences, began to agitate for separation, and in 1857 became a separate town in all but probate privileges, for which latter she still looks to Willimantic.

The building of so many dams across the river ended the days of shad fishing. This had been a popular pastime for the old Windhamites in the first century of the town, and was the first attraction to the vicinity of "The Falls." Not a few enterprising fishermen used to catch shad from the Willimantic and take them to New Haven when the legislature was in session, and sell them for fifty cents a pound. Fish stories of the first magnitude have come down to us from those old days, but I will eschew fiction and mention only one fact, which proves that handsome shad were caught in the Willimantic as late as 1830.

Robert Brown, the veteran real estate agent, tells me that he recalls sitting under an old tree in front of 'Squire Howes's blacksmith shop near the "Iron Works bridge," one morning in June, 1830, while his father went to the river with three other men, at a point near the end of the present No. 2 mill, to seine for shad; and in a short time they drew the net and caught thirty-one shad, weighing from three to five pounds each. They hauled frequently during the rest of the morning, but got only one more, and at noon they divided, eight shad each, and went home. Robert recalls that his father had some fresh-made butter in a pail to deliver at the store, and it was left standing in the sun during the fishing trip, to its great disadvantage, and his father got a sharp talking to when he got home; which incident is mentioned to show that men and women were much the same in those days as now.

When the great dam at Greeneville, near Norwich, was constructed, the builders agreed to place a certain number of shad above the dam each year, so as to keep the Shetucket and upper rivers supplied; but it appears that they used to comply with the letter of the law by placing the shad in a fish preserve above the dam, and then placing them in market for sale; and so the shad disappeared from the Willimantic by the greed of short-sighted speculators.

One of the most interesting recollections of early Willimantic appertains to the building of the upper bridge leading from the Columbia road to the Windham Co.'s mills. About 1830, Stephen Hosmer lived in the large white house still standing at the foot of Hosmer mountain, next east of the old Card road. He owned 500 acres or more of land, with a toll gate at either end, one on Post hill in Columbia and the other standing at the northwest side of what is now the junction of Bridge and Pleasant sts., and where the foundation remains of the old red tollgate house, only lately torn down, may still be seen. It used to cost six cents for a single toll when on business, but one could pass free to mill or to meeting; while for $1 a year, free passage at all times was allowed. The building of the Windham Company's settlement and Deacon Lee's plant made quite a village in that section and a demand arose for a bridge to reach it from Lebanon and Columbia without going away down around by the Iron Works Bridge. The fight for that bridge was a vigorous one. The town did not want to bear the expense. Appeal to the courts was taken and a special commission, after vigorous hearings, ordered the bridge. It was a wooden structure of course, and it was not until 1868 that the present substantial stone arch was built by Lyman Jordan. The lower stone arch, by the way, was also built by Lyman Jordan and Norman Melony, in 1857. The story goes that Lebanon was a little longer-headed than Windham when she surrendered her shad-fishing privileges in return for being released from Windham, thereby escaping a share of the expense of building the many bridges that stage-coach development and the growth of manufactures demanded.

HOUSE BUILT BY COL. ELDERKIN FOR HIS SON.

Many stories are told of the wealth that might have been this one's or that one's if he had only held the land in Willimantic now covered by costly buildings, but it is to be considered that had the land been held the buildings would not have appeared! But some did hold land to great advantage in early Willimantic. One of the best illustrations is the case of Jesse Spafford, who, shortly before 1820 and the appearance of the factories, was settling an estate, and he set off to one of the heirs, as equivalent to $100 in value, a strip of unoccupied land stretching alongside the Willimantic river and south of the turnpike (now Main street) from about opposite the Hooker house to E. A. Buck's present steam mill. The heir in question grumbled at the allotment and Spafford offered him his choice of the land, or $100 in cash, Spafford to take the land. The short-sighted heir seized the cash and Spafford took the land. Shortly afterwards came the factories, then the railroads, with the depot located on the Spafford tract. General L. E. Baldwin bought of Spafford the Franklin hall site, paying $600 for that alone. Spafford died worth about $40,000, practically all the outgrowth of his $100 tract.

THE BOROUGH.

In 1833 the Willimantic settlement had grown to a character of its own, as a manufacturing center distinct from Old Windham; and to conserve its own ends more directly, application was made for a Borough charter, which was granted by the legislature in 1833, through the efforts of Representative Stephen Hosmer. July 1st of that year, the first Borough election was held with the following result: Warden, Loring Carpenter; Burgesses, Wightman Williams, Asa Jillson, Samuel Barrows, Jr., Wm. C. Boon, Dr. William Witter, Royal Jennings, Elisha Weaver, Dr. Newton Fitch; Bailiff, Stephen Dexter. A tax was levied and Thomas Cunningham was appointed Collector.

THE OLD STATE MILITIA.

Among the most interesting of memories are those of the old "Training Days." Company trainings were held the first Mondays in May and September of each year.

All men between the ages of 18 and 45 were obliged to do training duty, unless they had some reasonable excuse. The military or commutation tax takes the place of this system to-day.

Training days were made gala occasions. "The Plains"—that smooth stretch of land at the foot of the hill, west of the Center—were the scene of the regimental trainings.

The farmer's motive for quick and early planting in May and for quick and early harvesting in September, was to get done in time for training day.

The Windham Rifle Company was organized in 1828, with Henry Hall as Captain. The members of the company attained a high degree of soldierly proficiency and dignity which nothing but the old Hebard tavern banquets could overcome. July 4th, 1829, the company was presented with a handsome silk banner by the ladies of Willimantic, and the ladies were entertained at Hebard's tavern. The company served as special guard in Brooklyn August 31st, 1829, at the hanging of Watkins the murderer, the last public execution in Connecticut.

Successive captains of the company were David Smith, Wm. L. Jillson, John H. Capen, John S. Jillson, Lloyd E. Baldwin, Edwen S. Fitch, Wm. B. Hawkins, Pearl L. Peck, Rensalaer O. Hovey. They disbanded in 1847, when the State militia system was changed. The greatest event of Windham in militia times was the great field drill inspection of the 5th Brigade Conn. Militia Sept. 29th and 30th, 1846, at Windham. Spectators were gathered from miles around and from all parts of the State. Gen. L. E. Baldwin was in command, and about 2000 privates and officers were assembled on the Green. Major Gen. Amos Fowler of Lebanon was reviewing officer, William Swift was aide, and the Rev. Horace Winslow was chaplain. Three of these men, Messrs. Baldwin, Swift and Winslow, are here at the bi-centennial celebration to-day. General Fowler still lives, in Lebanon.

WINDHAM'S CHURCHES.

The opening of the second century finds Old Windham's churches in the last stages of the Separatist or Sectarian agitation, and the old-time united loyalty and obligation to a common church and creed were never to return. It was now settled that any person could worship according to the dictates of conscience, but it was still obligatory to worship somewhere, or at least to pay taxes for the support of some religious institution. The venerable Reverends White at the Green, and Cogswell at Scotland, were sorely perplexed by these difficulties, and found it impossible to preserve harmony. Mr. White died in 1793, and young Elijah Waterman came from Bozrah to succeed him. His youth attracted many to him for a time, but he began a vigorous crusade against the prevailing heresies. Finally a portion of the liberals "certificated" themselves away to form an Episcopal society, and they had the Rev. John Tyler of Norwich, for an occasional preacher. They thus escaped paying taxes to Mr. Waterman's church, which was thereby sadly crippled, so that he resigned in 1805, and no settled pastor came again till 1808. Then the Rev. Mr. Andrews undertook the troublous task, but to no avail, and he requested dismissal, which was granted him in 1813. The next incumbent, Rev. Cornelius B. Everest, ordained in 1815, proved a man of superior tact, and the church became more united, and there were even accessions. He was much favored, of course, by the new era of religious liberty under the constitution of 1818, by which the old tax obligations to the church were abolished, and people were left free as now to sustain the church or not, as they chose. Mr. Everest remained until 1827, when he was succeeded by the Rev. R. F. Cleveland of Norwich, father of him who has since become famous as

President Grover Cleveland. This was Mr. Cleveland's first pastorate, and soon after he was ordained he went to Philadelphia and brought back a bonny bride to share his new responsibilities. They are remembered as very agreeable young people. Two of the children were born here, but not the future president. It is recalled that Mr. Cleveland was fond of horse-back riding. His ministry was quite successful, lasting three years. In 1828 Deacon Lee and a number of others withdrew to join the newly formed church at Willimantic. No settled pastor was again ordained until the Rev. J. E. Tyler came in 1837.

The other pastors since Mr. Tyler, who resigned in 1851, have been Revs. Geo. I. Stearns, Samuel Hopley, Hiram Day, A. F. Keith, Frank Thompson, F. A. Holden, W. S. Kelsey, F. M. Wiswall, the last named having just resigned. Four buildings have served the church, the present structure having been dedicated in 1887. The first church of Windham has sent out four strong churches from her loins, to Mansfield, Hampton, Scotland, Willimantic, besides others minor.

The first attempt to form an Episcopal Society in 1803, did not gain a foothold. In 1832, however, a permanent society was formed, and in 1833 the present church was built. The first rector was Rev. L. H. Corson, who recently died in Michigan; then William A. Curtis, Charles Todd, John W. Woodward, Henry B. Sherman, Giles N. Deshon, Abel Nichols, A. Ogden Easter, Joseph Brewster, Harry Edwards, Sanford J. Horton (who started here a select school for boys and took them with him to Cheshire), John H. Anketell, Alfred H. Stubbs, Clayton Eddy, E. W. Saunders, and since the establishment of St. Paul's mission at Willimantic, the rectors there have officiated at Windham, as will appear in my subsequent reference to the Willimantic mission. The present number of communicants in the Windham Episcopal parish is 23; connected with parish 61.

One of the Separatist organizations in Old Windham was

a Baptist society, which we find at the beginning of the second century in charge of Elder Benjamin Lathrop, who was chosen to the Legislature chiefly on that issue.

Over at North Windham, Joshua Abbe led another Baptist sect, called the Abbe-ites. Little other than missions have ever been maintained at North or South Windham. Attempts at regular church organization have been feeble and short lived. After Elder Lathrop's death, the Baptists at the Green were weakened and scattered for a time, but soon rallied and held meetings in Andrew Robinson's great kitchen, with various preachers, including Lorenzo Dow and Roger Bingham, but after the constitution of 1818, and the abolition of the church tax, these meetings died out. There was another Baptist organization on the Green about 1846, but it was short lived and its members drifted to Willimantic and Mansfield. In 1850, this church was changed to Presbyterian, but soon disbanded. The old church was sold and removed to Bolton for a Baptist church, and was afterwards burned.

In Willimantic, the Congregational church was organized in 1827. Dennis Platt, a Yale theologue, was the first pastor. Its first church, now made over into the Meloney Block, opposite the Hooker House, was built in 1828. Rev. Ralph S. Crampton of Madison was the next pastor, then came Philo Judson of Woodbury, then the Rev. Andrew S. Sharpe, who served for nine years. November 8th, 1846, the Rev. Samuel G. Willard entered upon a long and successful ministry of nineteen years. Mr. Willard was a staunch friend of education, taking active interest in the public schools, was acting visitor for many years, and his scholarly attainments won him a place among the Fellows of Yale College.

He was succeeded in 1869 by the Rev. Horace Winslow, who remained twelve years and was chiefly instrumental in getting the society to build the new church at the corner of Walnut and Valley streets, dedicated in May, 1871. After Mr. Winslow, came two popular acting pastors, but not ordained, Rev. S. R. Free and C. P. Crofts, and in

December, 1890, the present pastor, Rev. C. A. Dinsmore, was ordained. The church has 225 members.

The Baptist church was the first one organized in Willlimantic, Oct. 20th, 1827. The Rev. Chester Tilden was first pastor. They first held meetings in school houses, but hot prejudices barred them out. Their first structure was dedicated in 1829, on the site of the present one. It was sold to the Catholics in 1857, and the present building, since much enlarged and improved, was then built.

The pastors since Mr. Tilden have been Alfred Gates, Alva Gregory, Benajah Cook, John B. Guild, L. W. Wheeler, Thomas Dowling, Henry Bromley, Cyrus Miner, Henry R. Knapp, Edward Bell, Jabez Swan, E. D. Bentley, E. S. Wheeler, G. R. Damon, P. S. Evans, W. A. Fenn, Geo. W. Holman, M. G. Coker, J. B. Lemon.

The church has now about 400 members on its roll. The late Deacon A. H. Fuller was closely identified with it for many years, donating its handsome pipe organ.

The Methodists organized in Willimantic about the same time. Some of them held class meetings as early as 1825. The Rev. Mr. Gardner came and preached in the west school house about 1826, and in September, 1829, the first M. E. church was built, on the present site of the Atwood Block. The Rev. Horace Moulton was the first pastor.

The present church was begun in 1850, but has since been thoroughly modernized in its interior. The parsonage on Prospect street was built in 1868, before that street was built, and was then thought to be almost in the wilderness. The numerous itinerant pastors have been since 1828: Daniel Fletcher, H. Ramsdell, P. Townsend, E. Beebe, George May, J. E. Raisley, Hebron Vincent, K. Ward, Moseley Dwight, Philetus Green, S. Leonard, H. Horbush, Reuben Ransom, Pasdon A. C. Wheat, F. W. Bill, Chas. Noble, John Cooper, Daniel Dorchester, A. Robinson, Jonathan Cady, N. P. Alderman, Geo. W. Rogers, Chas. Morse, Wm. Purington, John Livesey, Wm. Kellen, E. B. Bradford, Geo. W. Brewster, Edgar F.

Clark, Geo. E. Reed, Chas. S. McReading, Shadrach Leader, Geo. W. Miller, S. J. Carroll, Wm. T. Worth, A. J. Church, S. McBurney, D. P. Leavitt, Eben Tirrell, C. W. Holden, A. P. Palmer, the present pastor.

In connection with the Methodist church, the Willimantic camp ground should be mentioned. Started in 1860, it at first grew in popular favor in a manner quite different from what its projectors intended, and the annual summer meetings became after a time, the rendezvous for thousands of pleasure seekers, and with the crowd there flocked to Willimantic and along the road to the grounds, a horde of hucksters or horse traders, to the equal annoyance of the association and the borough. "Right away to camp" became the annual shibboleth of a crowded, lively and sometimes boisterous week in Willimantic. But the association firmly pursued the even tenor of its way, developing the grounds as intended, and in later years the popular furore over camp-meeting has given place to gatherings in keeping with the place. There are to-day about 200 cottages and tents there, many families finding it a quiet, wholesome summer resort for weeks at a time, and the annual religious meetings in August are largely attended. The crowds that used to flock to Willimantic have disappeared, and camp-meeting is orderly and circumspect. Many distinguished Methodist preachers are heard at the grounds.

The Rev. Father H. Brady, then resident priest at Middletown, opened the first Catholic mission in Willimantic, in Franklin Hall in 1848, with about 300 in attendance. He purchased the land where the present church stands on Jackson street. The Rev. Bernard McCabe of Danielsonville, had charge of Willimantic mission until 1857. In later years he purchased the Baptist building and removed it to the site of the present church, christening it St. Joseph's Roman Catholic church. The Catholics, like the Baptists, but more severely, suffered persecution in their early days here. One Sunday Father McCabe found Franklin Hall locked against him, and the key nowhere to be found. Nothing daunted, he promptly led his flock to the then lately-purchased lot on Jackson street, and there under God's free dome he erected a rough altar, and offered up the adorable sacrifice. Another time he started to drive to Baltic, when suddenly a wheel came off and he was thrown violently to the ground. Examition showed that some scoundrel had removed all the nuts.

Father McCabe died in 1860, and was succeeded by the Rev. Hugh J. O'Reilly, who became the first resident pastor. In 1861 he built the present pastoral residence and also purchased the land for a Catholic cemetery, just beyond the Horse-shoe bridge.

The Rev. Daniel Mullen succeeded Father O'Reilly, and after four years was succeeded by the present incumbent, the Rev. Florimond DeBruycker. Father DeBruycker had under his charge when he first came here missions at Stafford Springs, Bolton and Coventry.

In 1864 he purchased the new Catholic cemetery, and in 1883 the old wooden church, (bought of the Baptists) was removed to Valley street, where it is now a part of the parochial school property, and on the site of the old church he erected the beautiful structure of brick and stone at a cost of $80,000, including the high altar, which was brought from Munich. The corner stone was laid August 17, 1875, by the late Bishop McFarland, his last official act. November 17, 1874, came the dedication led by the Rev. Bishop McQuade of Rochester. Our Catholic population is from 3500 to 4000 including about 1500 to 1800 French Canadians.

St. Paul's Episcopal Mission at Willimantic was organized about thirty years ago and the late Dr. Hallam was placed in charge. Meetings were long held in the upper hall of the Commercial block, afterwards in Dunham Hall. The present church was built in 1883, the parsonage in '87. By the '91 report 258 persons are registered parishioners and 84 communicants. The rectors since Dr. Hallam are Revs. R. K. Ashley, L. H. Wells, R. C. Searing, H. B. Jefferson, George Buck. All officiated at Windham also.

A Reform church was organized in 1881 in connection with the Willimantic Reform Society in Mission Hall, with Elder J. L. Barlow as pastor, but did not gain permanent foot-hold, and was disbanded in 1885. The Reform Society, organized in 1878, has since held weekly meetings, with the temperance question the chief topic of discussion.

Universalism has never gained a permanent foothold in this town. About 1840, a flourishing Universalist society was organized in Willimantic, a church was built on "Exchange Place," and the old church building is still standing, as a tenement house with basement stores, the third building east of Jackson street on Main street, and owned by George W. Burnham. Elder Harry Brown, a seceder from the Baptists, was a leader in this movement, and Whiting Hayden was the financial backer. The society flourished for a time, and out of it grew the present Spiritualist Society. The latter society has been active in Willimantic for about thirty years, in 1868 completed its church on Bank street, has maintained regularly its "Progressive Lyceum" every Sunday, and the church desk has been occupied by different speakers. George W. Burnham has been the leading spirit in this society, and is now also president of the State Spiritualist Society.

THE RAILROADS.

In 1849 the railroads came, and it was the biggest event of all.

Nothing will ever equal the first impression made by the iron horses. We have had since then the telegraph, the telephone and all the wonders of electricity, but they have come so thick and fast that we are now prepared for anything, and surprised at nothing.

The railroad had long been heralded, yet it was to most people an incomprehensible thing that the engine should go right along without anybody pushing or anything drawing, and no sign of a motive power but little puffs of smoke and steam.

It is reported—but I have not been able to fathom its accuracy—that one good old lady along the South Windham outskirts stood within hailing distance of the track one morning soon after the cars appeared, and waved her apron so frantically that the engineer stopped and asked her what the matter was. She inquired if they took "summer squashes."

As the first railroad appeared here in the fall, there is an apparent anachronism in the seasonableness of the squashes if not of the story.

The great "Air Line" was the first to be talked of and the last to be built. The first road appearing here was the New London, Willimantic and Palmer, now the New London Northern. The first train arrived here from Norwich in the fall of 1849, with an engine and two passenger cars. It stopped down back of John Moulton's house, and passengers were transferred by teams up to the place opposite Hardin Fitch's where the tracks from Palmer had reached. Large crowds were gathered at both points to see the sight.

It was several weeks later before the tracks were connected, but then a grand free excursion was given from New London to Palmer and a large number of people went along, General L. E. Baldwin among them.

The Hartford, Providence and Fishkill road came through in 1853. John F. Lester, the first station agent, met the first train from Hartford up near the Smithville Co's., before the depot was built, and is said to have sold the first tickets while standing by the track in the open air. William Storrs of Ashford, and before this date one of the teachers in the old stone school house, and to-day a wealthy director in the Reading Coal Co., in Scranton, Pa., became the agent of the New London Northern road. The depot was built in 1850, and did passenger service until 1880, when the present structure was built with the daily death trap of four tracks before it.

Nearly twenty years later the long agitated Boston, Hartford and Erie railroad, now main line of the New England, was completed from Boston to Willimantic, and in 1872. the New Haven, Middletown and Willimantic, (now the Air Line) entered the town, thus completing the quartet of railway outlets to all important points which make Willimantic to-day one of the most convenient and accessible railway centers in the country.

What Willimantic ought to have is a handsome new union passenger station, and I believe proper effort on the part of the citizens could induce the railroads to build it. The recent move of the Consolidated road makes the time opportune for united action. There too, on that magnificent location in front of the Windham Co's., is just the place for the union station. It would help both the town and the railroads in every way to build it. Such a move too, would give a fair chance for the prompt and convenient handling of freight in the present yard, and thus prove a great help to our mercantile interests.

The coming of the railroads broke up not only the stage coach business, but also the great teaming industry which preceded the modern freight traffic. The teaming thoroughfares from Willimantic led to Providence and Norwich, then our chief sources of supply. The Windham Company had a six horse team; Henry Brainard and Grant Swift were for many years their principal teamsters to Providence. Charles Huntington, the elder Ephraim Herrick and Martin Harris were among the teamsters to Norwich.

WINDHAM'S SCHOOLS.

Windham has always taken a good degree of interest in her schools. Early in her second century she had a good academy at the Green, and thirteen populous districts with well kept schools, and later, about 1850, Dr. Jabez Fitch maintained a very creditable academy at South Windham, known as the Grove Seminary, and the academy building is now standing on the hill east of the railway station and in the rear of the Warner House, being sometimes used for public gatherings. Several well-to-do citizens of the borough sent children to school there. Dr. Fitch was a very strict disciplinarian and demanded thoroughness of his pupils. An unfortunate occurrence resulting in the death of a young man whom he punished brought his labors here to a close. He afterwards went to South Norwalk and there built up a private school of considerable reputation, some Willimantic boys being sent there, and he conducted it until his death.

The first public school house built in the borough was in the Second District, and stood on the site where now stands the little cottage nearly opposite Charles B. Jordan's house on Pleasant street. Next was built a larger structure located on the north side of the river almost midway between the present spool shop and No. 1 mill. Then a two-story wooden structure was built a little west of what is now the Linen Co.'s dye house; and in 1831, near this same site, was built the famous "old stone school house" which was Willimantic's chief educational influence for nearly a generation, and is treasured in fond memory in many hearts here to-day assembled, and in many more that are widely scattered. Here are some of the sterling minds who taught Willimantic's young ideas how to shoot: Roger Southworth, Samuel L. Hill, Dr. Calvin Bromley, Dr. Eleazer Bentley, Wm. Kingsley, Robert Stewart, Leander Richardson, Wm. L. Weaver, Fred F. Barrows, Henry W. Avery, Harriet Moulton, Martha Chipman and Remus Robinson. The advent of the Linen Co. displaced this historic structure, and in 1865 the Second District took up its quarters in the Natchaug building as at present.

The first school house in the First District of Willimantic, stood about where the Windham Co.'s east dwelling house is on West Main street. This was a small building and was later removed to the lot now occupied by the First District buildings, and enlarged.

In 1847 the central and oldest building of the present three were built, and this, like the old stone school house in the Second District, served for many years as the educational center of that part of the town. In this district taught such sturdy pedagogues as John G. Clark, Horace Hall, Leonard R. Dunham, Dr. Wm. A. Bennett, Wm. L. Weaver, Saxton B. Little, E. McCall Cushman, Jabez S. Lathrop, Perry Bennett, John D. Wheeler.

For many years these two districts were rivals, but in 1887 came the union town High School, then in 1889 the State Normal Training School, with its model advantages for the First District grades, soon to be enjoyed also by the Second District grades.

I must not pass over the private High School maintained by David P. Corbin in Franklin Hall about 1862–'5. It was a school of high character, and attracted a large number of young men and young women from this and neighboring towns. Mr. Corbin followed Mr. Powell who was first principal of the new Natchaug school, and was himself succeeded by Thomas Hart Fuller, John B. Welch, Wm. L. Burdick and George A. Cadwell.

In the First District the principals since John D. Wheeler have been Wm. A. Holbrook, Chas. F. Merrill, Chas. F. Webster, Roderick W. Hine, Frank A. Young and F. A. Verplanck.

Frank H. Beede has been principal of the High School since its inception in 1887.

The Catholic parochial school was established in 1878, drawing about 200 pupils at that time from the public schools, chiefly in the Second District, and now numbering nearly 700 pupils, drawn from the families of Irish and French extraction in all parts of the town.

The reason for the establishment of parochial schools, here as elsewhere, was the absence of purely religious instruction in the public schools and the belief of Catholics that it should be given there.

The Protestants were thus made to realize also, that in

many instances too much of a Protestant bias had been given to the public schools.

At the present time there is a tendency toward making the parochial schools public. It is not generally believed wise to grant public money to parochial schools while they remain such, not because they are Catholic, but because it is felt to be unwise to maintain separate sectarian schools of any sort from the common fund. On the other hand, the patrons of the parochial schools, many of them tax-payers and all sharing directly or indirectly the burdens of the town, feel that they bear a double burden for schools when paying tuition at the parochial school. The new Faribault plan of Archbishop Ireland, by which parochial schools are to be committed under Catholic teachers to public charge but with no religious instruction save by Catholic missionaries at their own expense after regular school hours, may prove an entering wedge for an harmonious settlement of the whole matter.

WINDHAM IN WAR.

The war of 1812 was unpopular in Windham as among Federalists generally throughout the north, but quite a number of young Windahmites enlisted nevertheless, attracted by love of adventure and good pay.

Windham sailors had been impressed into British service. That sturdy little coasting frog, "The Windham," had been seized and confiscated, and these incidents gave the town a special interest in the struggle. Yet the Federalist influence was so strong that comparatively few enlisted at the beginning of the war. A number of young fellows from the Center and from Scotland Parish saw a week's delightful service in "guarding" New London Harbor, but they saw no fighting.

Windham was well represented in the regular army, however, at the time this war broke out, by Major Charles Larrabee, Capt. Adam Larrabee and Col. Staniford. Of the last named I can learn but little, save that he was a young and popular officer. Major Charles Larrabee was a Windham boy, but had been on the western frontier for a number of years. He served under Gen. Harrison, whom he well knew, and he also had personal association with Gen. Zachary Taylor and Winfield Scott. Capt. Adam Larrabee was a grandson of Timothy Larrabee, of whom we have already heard. He was born and reared in Ledyard, was educated at West Point, and entered the regular army. At the battle of French Mills, near Plattsburg, on the northern frontier under General Wilkinson, his captain was disabled, and young Larrabee was placed in command, but was soon severely wounded, shot through the lung. He was carried from the field as fatally shot, but he rallied. The physician who examined him said, "Well, Larrabee, you're a queerly made fellow. If your heart were where it ought to be, you'd be dead by this time." "My heart, doctor," promptly explained the gallant young officer with a significant twinkle in his eye, "I left at home in Ledyard." He was taken to the home of the late Reuben H. Walworth (afterwards State Chancellor) at Saratoga and while recuperating there formed a lifelong friendship with the distinguished New Yorker. At the close of the war, young Larrabee, who inherited strong affection for home and family, made up his mind that the army was no place for him, so he threw up the captain's commission which he had earned by brave service, returned home and claimed the hand of her who had his heart in keeping (Hannah G. Lester) and settled down to farming in old Ledyard, where for forty years his farm was the model of thrift and intelligent agriculture. In later life he removed to Windham, and many now living recall him. His sons, Charles and Henry, are well known residents of Windham.

I do not learn that Windham was especially interested in the Mexican war, but our late distinguished citizen, Col. Rufus L. Baker, was chief of ordinance during that struggle, though not a resident of Windham until after that date. His son Chas. L. Baker, who lived here, was later connected with the regular army.

Oh, those days of '61 ! How little we to whom they are history, or but the dimmest memory, can realize what they meant to you who were in and of them ! Windham was alive at the outset to the country's needs. From the fall of Richmond she took keen interest in the struggle and gave freely of her blood and her substance for the union. Lester E. Braley was the first to enlist, joining the first company of Connecticut Volunteers, and he afterwards helped to raise and became captain of the "Lyon Guards", (Co. G. 12th C. V.)

Other well-known Windham boys who went to the front were Chas. D. Bowen, (Capt. Co. H. 18th C. V.) Francis S. Long, first lieutenant, and captain of Co. D. 21st C. V., who fell at Petersburg in '64, the gallant officer for whom our local G. A. R. Post is named. At the time he was killed he was in the command of the Brigade sharpshooters.

Henry E. Taintor, now of Hartford, was second lieutenant Co. H. 18th C. V.; Wm. H. Locke, Sergeant and second lieutenant 18th C. V; the patriotic Ripley Brothers, four of them in the service, of whom Eleazer H. became captain Co. D. 8th C. V., came back with an empty sleeve and is now in the civil service at Washington; Andrew Loomis, lieutenant Co. H. second C. V.; all of whom went out from Willimantic. Samuel J. Miller went to Virginia and enlisted there. Joel R. Arnold received commission as lieutenant and aide on the colonel's staff of 165th N. Y. Lieutenant Chas. Wood, a popular Willimantic boy, was killed at Petersburg in '64. Dr. Lathrop of Windham gave his life for the boys in the hospital and was brought to the historic old Windham cemetery. On his shaft erected by the 8th C. V., are the words, "Faithful Unto Death."

In all, 304 enlisted from Windham during the war in twenty-two different regiments, of whom fourteen were killed, twenty-five died, thirty-nine were wounded and

THE FROG POND.

thirty-two, alas, deserted. Benajah E. Smith, now worthy state commander, enlisted from Windsor in 1862, and Captain Charles Fenton, now of General Alger's staff, and Captain Jerome B. Baldwin, went out from Mansfield.

John Bolles, the veteran letter carrier, whose stirring drum beats have inspired many a loyal heart, went out from old Ashford, and James Haggerty of the present Court of Burgesses, was one of the youngest, if not actually the youngest, to enlist from Connecticut. He went out from Willimantic in Co. H, 18th C. V., Jan. 5, 1863, being then thirteen years, one month and eleven days old.

Many things happened to bring the people of Windham into close touch with the war. Troops passed through here frequently by rail, and the battalions of General Burnside and Governor Sprague of Rhode Island aroused special interest. General Wool. one of the veterans of the Mexican campaign, also passed through here.

But the event which brought the realization of the war to Windham County and all her towns was the death and funeral of our own beloved General Nathaniel Lyon, who fell in that gallant charge at Wilson's Creek, Aug. 10th, 1861, at the very outset of the struggle. The body was brought to his old home in Eastford, and with its distinguished escort, and greeted with signs of sincere popular mourning in its long journey from Missouri, reached Willimantic on the morning of Wednesday, Sept. 4th, by special train. Thousands of people had come together from miles around, the procession was formed and moved to the outskirts, where carriages were in waiting. Samuel J. Miller and John Henney tolled the Methodist bell as the solemn train moved to the north.

The next day came the funeral at Eastford, business was generally suspended, and Willimantic, like all the surrounding towns, was fairly deserted, so many attended. It was a deeply impressive occasion, and aroused a profoundly patriotic spirit throughout the whole region.

I well remember the closing days of the war. First

came the joyous news of the fall of Richmond, when bells rang and cannons boomed. Young and old displayed the national colors. My own special delight was in a tiny flag worn proudly in the hat or carried running in the breeze—we little folks had them, we knew not really why, but we knew and felt that some great joy was at hand.

Then came the sudden plunging into deepest grief, our little flags were trimmed with crepe, and the church bells tolled, and solemn services were held, men and women wept like children. The great grief hangs even now like a heavy pall over my childhood's memory, though I knew not what it meant. They said the President was dead, shot by the hand of a traitor, a martyr to the cause of liberty and the Union.

I remember, too, when the "boys in blue" came marching home—boys in faded blue, with garments war-worn, flags tattered and faces haggard. I can see them now, as though it were but yesterday, standing there on Union Street, in front of the Baptist Church, where we children attended lovely Rose Dimock's private school in the vestry, and though the spectacle was to our childish minds simply one of awe and wonder, we felt that somehow those men had suffered. Another memory, quite as vivid, is that some of the soldiers in mock menace "charged bayonets" upon our ranks, and we fled in terror to the protection of "teacher."

NORTH AND SOUTH WINDHAM.

By the kindness of Mr. P. H. Woodward, a native of Franklin, son of the late Ashbel Woodward, M. D. and who is now secretary of the Hartford Board of Trade and an active member of the Connecticut Historical Society, I am able to present the following facts concerning the manufacturing settlements at North Windham and South Windham. Much of the material, which was gleaned from original sources by Mr. Woodward, is now for the first time published.

North Windham.—About the year 1810, the firm of Taintor, Abbe & Badger (John Taintor, Charles Taintor, George Abbe and Edmund Badger) built a paper mill at North Windham, then known as "New Boston." Previously, the water power at this place had been utilized only for driving a saw mill. They made writing paper of three grades respectively, No. 1, No. 2 and No. 3. The texture was firm and strong, but the finish inferior. The Taintor Brothers and George Abbe were merchants of Windham Center. To a large extent help was paid and stock purchased through orders on neighboring traders, who in this way bartered for the products of the mill, money playing a small part comparatively in effecting the exchanges.

After a few years of doubtful success the other partners prudently retired, leaving Badger alone in nominal ownership. About the year 1825 he failed, when the property practically reverted to the Taintors, by virtue of claims upon it.

For a short period after the withdrawal of Badger, a new firm, Foster & Post, ran the mill, but from lack of capital or encouragement, soon abandoned the business.

Meanwhile, one Pickering, an Englishman, had shipped to this country a Fourdrinier machine, the first imported in America. It was sent from London by way of Germany on account of certain duty regulations. On the passage hither the owner entrusted the care of the machine to two fellow countrymen of his, coming himself by another vessel direct. On the voyage a severe epidemic broke out, so prostrating both passengers and crew, that the craft was with difficulty brought into port. Pickering attributed the preservation of his life to the fidelity of his servant, John Carter, an Irishman, one of a very few that escaped the disease.

He soon formed a partnership with Mr. Frost, a Boston bookseller, under the name of Frost & Pickering. In seeking a location they finally selected North Windham. The old mill had become dilapidated, but was in the market at low figures, and this was probably the inducement which determined their choice.

The new firm took possession in 1827. The structure was in a great measure rebuilt, under the supervision of George Spafford of South Windham, an experienced mill wright.

Notwithstanding the superiority of the new machine, misfortunes continued to pursue the enterprise. Pickering is represented as a dashing man, more devoted to jolly companionship than to work. A similar disposition prevailed among the employees. As a set they were intemperate and consequently indifferent. The inevitable catastrophe in due time followed, bankruptcy again stopping the wheels in 1829.

Grant & Daniels, Boston creditors of Frost & Pickering, then operated the mill for about two years, but managed its affairs at arms' length, with unsatisfactory results.

In 1831 the property was sold to Justin Swift, Charles Taintor having foreclosed the mortgage which he had held from the time when it passed into the hands of Edmund Badger. Mr. Swift converted the concern into a cotton mill, and supervised the business personally till 1860. At his advent the train of disasters that had for twenty years involved successive operators in trouble, happily came to an end. Applying to the work, industry, capacity and integrity he succeeded in making money where others had failed.

The mill was burned in 1837 and again in 1860, and in both instances rebuilt. The second rebuilding was in 1862, and it was then leased to Merrick Bros. for thread making. In 1872 it was bought by E. H. Hall & Son. E. H. Hall died in 1884, and the son, E. H. Hall, Jr., buying out the heirs, has since continued the business under the old firm name. Forty hands are now employed in the manufacture of cotton yarns, the finished product amounting to 3000 pounds per week, making a yearly product of about $40,000 value.

At the instance of Mr. Pickering, Mr. Stowell Lincoln

who owned a fulling mill at North Windham, began about the year 1827 to make the felts that were required in operating the Fourdrinier. After the general introduction of this machine he continued to make them for the trade till 1857, when the appliances of the business were sold and transferred to South Windham. The factory is now unused and going to decay.

South Windham.—South Windham has earned a notable place in the history of manufactures. Its water power is derived from a stream draining "Pigeon Swamp," a watershed of perhaps four square miles on the eastern borders of Lebanon. The fall is quite remarkable, being over 150 feet from the upper reservoir now in use, to the place where it empties into the Shetucket.

Aside from a sawmill higher up, the power was first used for driving a fulling mill, located on the present site of the works of Smith, Winchester & Co. Cloth woven on hand looms was brought to this establishment not only from the neighborhood, but from places twenty or thirty miles distant, to be dressed, finished and dyed. During the last war with Great Britain the army cloth turned out here won a high reputation for the excellence of its indigo blue. From the hands of Joshua Smith the mill passed into the ownership of Geo. Spafford, and was demolished in 1829.

In the year 1800, Amos Denison Allen established the cabinet business at the old homestead near South Windham, where he continued to carry it on for about a third of a century. He was an excellent workman and very thorough. The products of his shop were distributed extensively through Eastern Connecticut and portions of Massachusetts. Many old fashioned long clock cases were made here for the southern market. At different periods from six to fourteen hands were employed.

Many pieces, embracing articles of rare and curious design, that have been in constant use from half to three fourths of a century, are still to be found in the neighborhood in excellent preservation. Chairs that have descended in the course of two generations from the parlor to the kitchen, as firm in every joint as when they left the maker, are still triumphantly exhibited in proof of the superiority of the old regimen in cabinet making to the new. Mr. Allen was born March 13, 1774 and died August 19, 1855.

Mr. Joseph Pickering imported the first "Fourdrinier" ever landed in the United States and located at North Windham in 1827. George Spafford of South Windham, a skillful mill-wright, was employed to rebuild the mill, which had fallen into decay, and to adapt it to the uses now required. While thus engaged he became impressed with the merits of the "Fourdrinier" and foresaw the revolution it was destined to accomplish. All paper previously manufactured in the United States had either been made by hand, or on the primitive cylinder machine, the product of which was much inferior to the hand-made.

The theory of making paper in a continuous web was first wrought out in 1779, by Louis Robert, a common workman of Ensonne, France. The Fourdrinier Brothers, (Henry and Lealy) wealthy booksellers of London, purchased the patent right for Great Britain in 1804. They not only improved the invention greatly, but also brought its utilities into general notice. It has since borne their name, and notwithstanding the wonderful development of mechanical ingenuity since their time, still remains the standard machine for the manufacture of all the finer grades of paper. In its modern completeness it is justly regarded as one of the greatest achievements of human contrivance.

Although it soon became apparent that from extrinsic causes the enterprise of Pickering was doomed to failure, Mr. Spafford, convinced that the Fourdrinier was destined to supersede the clumsy devices then in use, determined to begin the manufacture of them. Having at different places been brought into relations with Mr. James Phelps, a mechanic of wide experience in building paper mills, the two men formed a partnership for the purpose.

On the 8th of January 1829, Charles Smith, son of Joshua, then a youth of 21, went to Stafford (New Furnace) now Staffordville, to take charge of the business. Having supervised the building operations at North Windham he had become familiar with the mechanism of the Fourdrinier. Stafford was selected because a foundry was already established there where the castings could be made. The work was carried on in a loft, and ample precautions taken to protect the secrets of the undertaking from the knowledge of the public. Of course curiosity was rife and some laughable explanations were given to place it on an innocent scent.

The first Fourdrinier made on this continent was duly completed and sold to Amos H. Hubbard of Norwich, by whom it was put in operation in May, 1829, at "The Falls." A second quickly followed and was purchased by Henry Hudson of East Hartford. Both yielded such excellent results that the projectors were encouraged to make preparations for the continuance of the business. Accordingly having removed their tools and a third Fourdrinier from Stafford, they broke ground for a shop on the site of the old fulling mill at South Windham, Nov. 30, 1829. The building was ready for occupancy in February, 1830.

They were the pioneers not only in building the Fourdriniers, but also in many other cardinal improvements. In 1831 the first dryers produced in this country were made in this shop. Hitherto each American paper mill was provided with an airy loft wherein the fresh sheets were suspended by hand till their moisture evaporated. By means of the dryers the same result was accomplished automatically, thus effecting a great saving both in space and labor. Soon after Mr. George Spafford invented the cutter for dividing the continuous web into sheets of uniform size, a contrivance hardly inferior to the dryers in its economic bearings.

Phelps & Spafford built numerous paper mills for customers in different states and supplied them with machinery. The country was then comparatively poor, each Fourdrinier costly, and bad debts numerous. As the hard times of 1837, so painfully noted in our annals for financial disasters, approached, the strain upon the resources of the firm became too severe to be successfully withstood. The partners sold their interest to Charles Smith and Harvey Winchester, both brothers-in-law of George Spafford. In 1838 the new organization was completed under the name of Smith, Winchester & Co., the name which it still bears, Mr. Smith taking the general management.

By the death of his father Mr. Smith was left an orphan at the age of thirteen, when the duties cares and responsibilities of manhood at once devolved upon him. Before attaining his majority he directed the operations of large gangs of men, proving equal to every task as it came. Uniting rare executive ability to mechanical talent both natural and cultivated of a high order, he started the concern upon a career of prosperity which it has since pursued undeviatingly through all the ups and downs of the general business of the country. It has been a fundamental rule of the establishment to knowingly permit none but first class work to leave its doors, while the integrity of its dealings has won the confidence of its patrons.

Since 1838 the works have been several times enlarged, and commodious out buildings for storing lumber, patterns, etc., erected. Above the "fulling mill pond" two large reservoirs have been built, the last 150 feet above the bed of the Shetucket and flowing over 35 acres, having been begun in the autumn of 1877. Aside from supplies for the home market, machinery has been made here on orders from Canada, Cuba, Mexico, England and other foreign countries. At present the works have a capacity for the employment of about one hundred hands. In the quality of its productions the firm has always aimed at durability, strength and efficiency.

South Windham is also entitled to the credit of revolutionizing the cutting of wood type and multiplying many fold the demand for these useful articles by increased cheapness and excellence. Until Mr. Edwin Allen entered the field, wood type had been cut exclusively by hand and was so inferior in design and finish that even in the large sizes metal was generally preferred. Edwin Allen, son of Amos D., was born March 27, 1811. Having served an apprenticeship in his father's shop where he introduced several valuable inventions of his own, he moved to Norwich in 1835, to assist an elder brother in cabinet-making. The following year the factory was burned. While out of employment he strolled into the printing office of the Norwich "Courier," when he became suddenly interested in a font of wood type. Having made numerous inquiries in reference to their cost, utility, manufacture and other cognate points, he left for home inspired with the belief that machinery could be devised for making them. Although in delicate health he devoted his entire energies to the evolution of the idea that had seized him. The thought triumphed. In the short period of three days it had become embodied in wood and iron, for in that brief interval a small machine had been contrived which produced specimens far superior to any ever exhibited before. He returned to South Windham to begin the cutting of wood type for the general market.

In the spring of 1837 he visited New York City where he entered into an arrangement with Mr. George F. Nesbitt who undertook to introduce the article to the trade of the country. It was brought out as "Nesbitt's wood type," and was thus known for years.

Mr. Allen was able not only to devise and make the machinery even to the tempering of the steel cutting apparatus so that it would take the most exquisite edge needful for the purpose, but also to draft the letters of the whole alphabet to correspond with any specimen that might accompany an order. Many of his designs won great admiration as specimens of art.

The first effect of the invention was to drive inferior products out of the business, and to stimulate the rest to higher excellence. Prior to 1837 a large proportion of wood type were cut on the side of the grain for the reason that the blocks were more easily chiseled on the side than on the end. Letters thus formed, however, left a poor, imperfect impression in printing and deteriorated rapidly with use. The leading firm then in the trade was Levingworth & Wells of New York city. Their choicer grades, though cut on the end and recognized as the best in the market, made but a poor exhibit beside the deep, sharp, smooth and true lines of the machine made work. It was not long before the competition of the old methods came to an end, leaving Mr. Allen in undisputed posssession of the field.

A second effect was the complete supersedure of large metal type, tons of which were now melted down and cast into small type, since their new rivals of wood were lighter, better, more durable, much less expensive, and not liable to be injured or to cause injury when falling or when pied.

It is a notable fact that the essential principle of the machine, born in the brain of the inventor during those three days of intense thought, though now in world-wide use, has never been altered or improved.

The one first constructed was run by foot. As the business increased a shop was fitted up for Mr. Allen in an outbuilding of Smith, Winchester & Co., power being conveyed across the highway by an underground shaft. A steam mill was subsequently built at the old homestead, which in 1852 or 1853 was moved to the stream.

While at South Windham, Mr. Allen invented and manufactured in large quantities the "Educational Tables," which combining instruction with amusement, once enjoyed wide popularity. In 1852 he sold his factory and fixtures at South Windham to Mr. John G. Cooley, who after a year or two transferred the business to New York city. Other inventions of Mr. Allen have been numerous and some of them very valuable.

Guilford Smith (son of Charles and grandson of Joshua) purchased the property in 1863 and still owns it. He made woolen felts till the disproportionate rise of the raw material during the war gave foreign a great advantage over home manufactures. He is now the active manager of the works of Smith, Winchester & Co.

Several journey-man wood type cutters leased the premises in 1878, and under the name of "The American Wood Type Co." re-established the business for which the mill was originally built. The quality of their work is said to be unsurpassed either in this country or abroad.

About the year 1837 a grist mill was built at the lower end of the village by Elisha Holmes. Since 1850, thousands of tons of gypsum, imported by the ship load from Nova Scotia, have been ground here and distributed over an extensive region to fertilize the soil.

In the year 1871 a brick mill driven by steam, was built near the depot of the New London & Northern railway, by "The Adams Nickel Plating and Manufacturing Co," the president of the company being the inventor of the process. After the expiration of the patent the property was bought by a coal company and is now used for the manufacture of buffing wheels.

WILLIMANTIC MANUFACTURES.

The second era of manufactures in Willimantic began with the advent of the Willimantic Linen Company. It is a familiar story, oft recorded, and I need not dwell upon it. The company was organized in 1854, "to manufacture flax or cotton into yarn or cloth." They occupied the old Jillson Mill (now the spool shop) the Jillsons having failed to establish their manufactures permanently, and the Linen Company first manufactured fine and coarse towels or crash, also fish lines.

The Crimean war of 1853-6 deprived them of flax, and they were compelled to abandon the linen enterprise; but under the same name they promptly turned their attention to spool cotton. Spool cotton was at that time all imported, and only black and white thread was wound on spools, the colored varieties being sent over in skeins. The little penny skeins of colored thread will be recalled by many. The company first made up a lot of colored threads wound on spools, of quality much inferior to the present make and even to the goods they imported, but brightly glazed, and put them on the market. The bright colors and the novelty and pride of home manufacture caught the public eye, and gave the new industry a good start. In 1857 the mill now known as No. 1 was built. Then came on the civil war. Dunham and Ives were shrewd enough to buy up large quantities of cotton before the rise, and they became very wealthy. The capital thus acquired was turned to good account in beginning the development of a great plant.

In 1864, they purchased the tract now covered by mill No. 2 and its adjuncts; and the "old stone school house," the blacksmith shop, and the grist mill of earliest Willimantic gave way to progress.

The whole section round about was revolutionized, the "New Village," or large group of tasty tenement houses opposite the mills was built, and a new era dawned for Willimantic.

The "new mill" was the wonder of modern Windham, marking the advent of our greatest industry, and the forerunner of growth to a large town. In 1876, the old Jillson and Capen Mill (now No. 3) was acquired by purchase, and filled up with new machinery. Feb. 28, 1880, the building of No. 4 mill was authorized by vote of the directors. The next day, March 1st, the workmen were cutting away trees and digging for the foundations. The pines then growing in the Florida forests were speedily selected for the lumber of the mill, and so rapidly was the great structure pushed that on the first day of October following it began turning out products. This feat was characteristic of the company's enterprise. "The Oaks" settlement of cottages was built to accompany this mill.

The development of this company has materially affected the whole process of thread manufacture, by means of the improvements which its enterprise stimulated. Two notable inventions, the winding and ticketing machines, which act with almost voluntary power, were generally adopted by other thread companies which paid royalties to the Willimantic company until other improvements were introduced.

The Willimantic Company claims to make the best thread in the world, has sustained the claim by winning the first medals at the Philadelphia and Atlanta Expositions, and looks confidently forward to beating the world again at Chicago in 1893. Latterly other branches of manufacture have been introduced by this company, notably the lisle thread industry, which has been quite a feature for six months past, but was a sort of temporary "fad," and is now giving way to the manufacture of certain varieties of fancy yarns.

The employees now number about 2000, and the total yearly product is about fifteen millions of miles of threads and yarns.

Old Windham has a tradition of the revolutionary war, telling how Hettie's pet black cosset Dido was shorn of wool one morning, to make a suit of linsey-woolsey for Hettie's soldier brother, who was to leave next morning early to rejoin his company on the memorable march of the winter of '77-'78, from Rhode Island to New Jersey; and that the next morning after the wool was shorn, the proud young patriot was wearing his new suit, not 24 hours from Dido's back, so deftly had the hands of Hettie and the willing neighbors wrought.

Modern Windham has a story to match it, true beyond question. At the Atlanta Exposition of 1880, at the instance of our Linen Company, cotton growing in the boll in the fields in the morning, was picked, ginned, carded, spun, woven and dyed, and by the close of the same day was sewed by Willimantic thread and lined with Cheney silk, into two dress suits which were worn by the governor of the state and by Edward Atkinson, the distinguished economist, at a public reception that evening. The enterprise shown and the fame won at Atlanta developed a large southern trade for the company, which it still enjoys.

Next in importance to its cotton thread industry stands the silk industry of Willimantic, now fast assuming rank with the foremost.

After Col. Elderkin's death in old Windham, his silk industry passed into the hands of parties in Mansfield, the pioneer town of silk, and it is a curious coincidence that the leading silk manufactory of later Mansfield should have drifted again to Windham, in the Willimantic field. I refer to the O. S. Chaffee company, which was organized in Mansfield as early as 1838, became O. S. Chaffee & Son in 1867, established itself in the old Paisley mill corner Church and Valley Streets in Willimantic in 1874, organized as the Natchaug Silk Company Dec. 5th 1887, with $25,000 capital, increased to $200,000 Aug. 27th, 1888, and is now located in the handsome new building on North Street, manufacturing braids, linings, dress silks, watch guards, eye glass cords and fish lines, which are sold all over the country; and employing about 225 hands. Sewing silks are still made at the old mills in Mansfield, but the new plant at Willimantic has far outgrown the old.

The first silk industry to locate in Willimantic, however, was that of the Holland Manufacturing Company, which was started in 1866 by J. H. and G. Holland, brothers of Dr. J. G. Holland of literary fame. They built the two brick mills now on the opposite corners of Church and Valley Streets. J. H. Holland built for his home the brick house on Maple Avenue now occupied by the Misses Brainard, and Goodrich Holland erected the residence at the corner of Church and Spring Streets now owned and occasionally occupied by his widow, Mrs. Jane Holland. J. H. Holland died in 1868, and Goodrich in 1870, and since that time the business has been conducted under the old firm name, with Samuel L. Burlingham as resident agent. The manufactures of these mills are machine twist, button-

hole twist and sewing silk. They employ 150 hands
Mr. Goodrich Holland was the inventor of the machine
for stretching silk now in universal use among manufacturers of twist and sewings.

The latest accession to the silk industries of Willimantic is Arthur G. Turner's four story brick spinning mill on Bank street. This industry was started in 1886, and entered its present mill in 1889, and during the past year has paid out over $25,000 in wages to about 100 hands. The business is that of spinning silk yarns, which are shipped for use in the manufacture of all kinds of silk fabrics, for sewing machines and for fringes.

One of the largest and most important industries of Willimantic to-day, employing about sixty skilled mechanics, is the W. G. & A. R. Morrison Machine Co., manufacturers of silk machinery. This company has grown out of a little machine shop started by Walter and Henry Morrison in 1875, and was organized as a joint stock company in 1882. They now occupy the wooden building at the corner of North and Valley streets, and the lower floor of the Natchaug silk mill. They manufacture machinery for making silk twist complete, from the stock as imported to the finished spool—also machinery for making organzine and tram, which constitute the warp and woof of silk dress goods; also machinery for putting the gloss on cotton thread and winding it on spools. The business is not covered by patents, but has only two or three competitors in this country, as it calls for special machinery, which is all designed by Mr. W. G. Morrison. The sales for the past year exceeded $100,000 in value, and were shipped from Maine to California.

Among the other industries of modern Willimantic, the old Windham Cotton Company is still doing business at the old stand, which it has occupied since 1823. The present product is both wide and narrow goods in cottons, and includes sateens, twills, sheetings and print cloths. The plant has been enlarged, and improved in many ways within the past few years the mills have been thoroughly renovated and repaired, and nearly all the machinery, including water wheels, engine and boilers, of new and modern type, so that hardly anything remains of the original mills, save the familiar walls and roof. About 300 hands are employed. A number of small, but important inventions, now in universal use, have been invented at this mill.

The Smithville Company has had a rather checkered existence. There have been long intervals of idleness there. At the present time a Providence Company are employing about 300 hands there, making twills and print cloths, and turning out a yearly product of 3,000,000 yards.

These comprise the leading manufactures of the Willimantic of to-day, besides which there are planers' and builders' mills, blind factories, several large lumber yards, and a host of business houses for all sorts of domestic supplies.

An Electric Light Company lights the streets and has applied for a street railway charter. A complete system of public water works, established in 1885, has already become practically self-sustaining, and its power may some day be utilized for the generation of electricity for lights and motive power, including a street railway. Willimantic expects to become a city in December, 1893.

WINDHAM IN REFORMS.

The interest of Windham in the Abolition agitation was intense, and one typical reminiscence is at hand. During President William Henry Harrison's administration 1840-44, Aaron Phelps attempted to give a course of three anti-slavery lectures in the old Methodist church on the site of the present Atwood Block, and when the Rev. Moses White was pastor. The first lecture passed off quietly. The second night a mob gathered, but spent their wrath on the church after the meeting was over, by

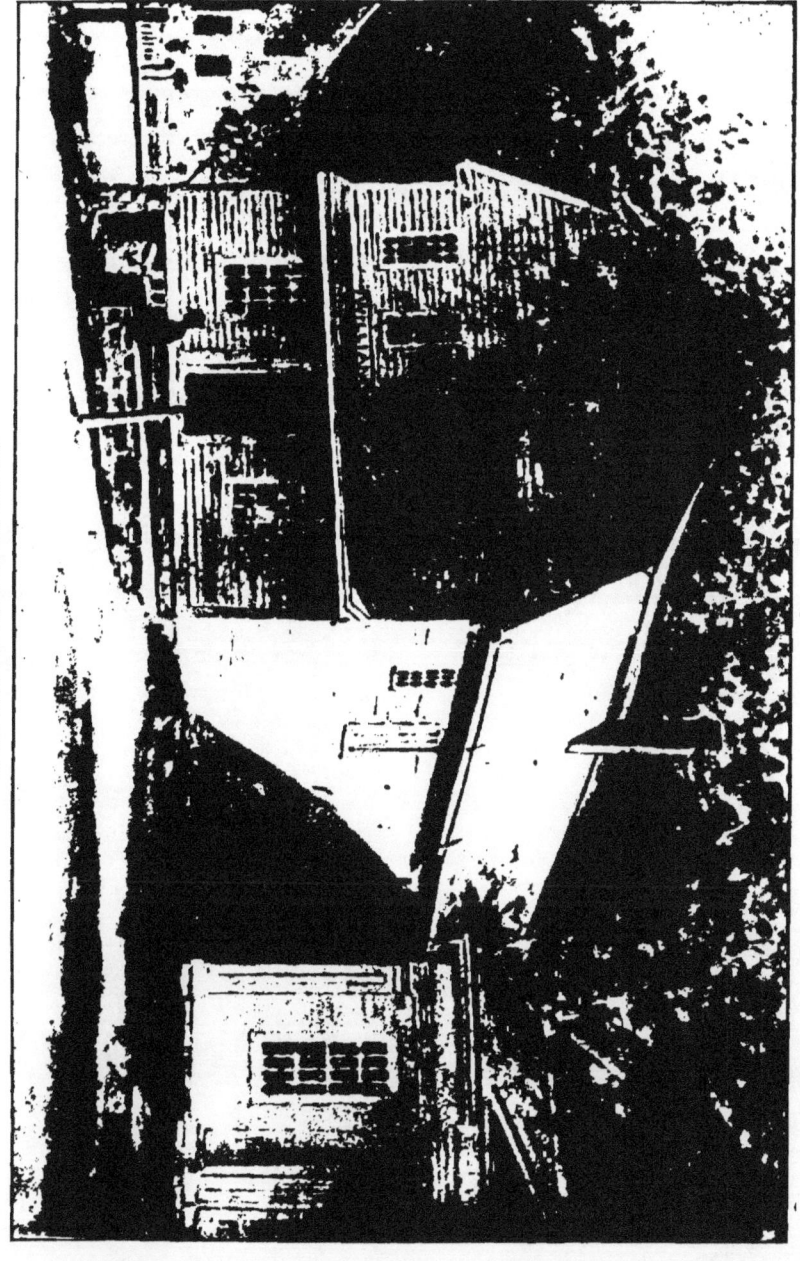

THE OLD SWIFT STORE AND POST OFFICE.
Formerly stood on site now occupied by Congregational church. Upper rooms used many years for Masonic Hall, and at one time as headquarters for the "Know-nothing" movement.

breaking windows, etc. The third night their proportions had grown to a well-organized mob, and as I am informed, they gathered at the Congregationalist church, and when the speaker was well under way, marched under the lead of Charles Schofield to the M. E. church. There Schofield approached the desk with followers, presumably to drag the speaker out, when young Orrin Robinson, tall and strong, interfered, and taking Schofield by the arm, quickly marched him back again through the crowd and into the street before the astonished mob had time to collect its wits sufficiently to know what was the matter. But the reaction soon came, and serious trouble was imminent. Edward Clark of Windham Green read the riot act, Robinson was arrested, tried and sentenced to a term in Brooklyn jail. Constable William H. Hosmer set out for Brooklyn with his prisoner, but finding he had forgotten necessary papers he requested young Robinson to walk on alone while he returned for the papers. Robinson trudged cheerily along, and when asked by one whom he met where he was going, promptly replied "to Brooklyn jail." He was soon overtaken by the constable and placed in durance vile. To return to the meeting which the mob had broken up, it is gratifying to add that Aunt 'Rushy Robinson cheated them of their victim, the speaker, by dressing him in her cloak and taking him to her home. Some of the leading citizens of the town took part in the mob. We are all quick now to condemn the bigotry of those old days. It is always the bigotry and intolerance of the present that we need to guard against.

Windham has never been a strong temperance town. From the days of Windham flip and West India wet goods, when "Bacchus" sat aloft as the type of the tavern's hospitality, down through the "Sodom" of early Willimantic, the orgies at the Hebard tavern, the killing of Calvin Robinson by a drunken driver, and the stabbing of the Corcoran boy at Mrs. Daley's, the pages of our history have been often blotted with the blood of the victims of alcohol. All along the years I find record of the wreck of some of the brightest minds in the community, because of the social popularity of drinking. The Washingtonian movement swept the town like wild-fire, as it did elsewhere, and wrought much good among individuals. The brilliant but unfortunate George S. Catlin, led in another temperance reform movement which profoundly stirred the people but did not exert a lasting influence. The Maine law had its day and for a time was very effective, but people expected too much of the law, and too little of themselves. Along in the '70s came the famous Good Samaritan movement, and moral enthusiasm ran high for a time with good effect. The great incentive force to intemperance in later days, has been the pernicious license system, introduced to restrict the evil, but proving instead a bulwark and a fostering influence. We are seeing a new light in this reform, shining from out the new scientific truths about alcohol. The intelligent man of to-day who will permit himself to recognize this truth, refuses to drink because he knows better than to cripple his physical and mental powers. In the public schools we teach the children these new truths, and in the family. But for some reason we have persisted in keeping the authority and influence of government against scientific truth and, social aspiration. During the past year we of Windham have made an attempt to place government in harmony with what we know our best interest as a community demands. Some ground has been gained, but a firmer effort is needed. It is a mistake to license or tolerate public vices in any form.

OLD WINDHAM OF TO-DAY.

The coming of railways robbed Windham Green of the last of her ancient glories—the stage coach and the prosperous tavern. The town clerk's office and probate records and the polling place were removed to Willimantic about 1862. The establishment of Willimantic Savings Institute in 1842 had brought into the field a formidable rival to the old Windham Bank, which since its establishment in 1832, had been the financial centre of the town. It was a novel thing for the people to have money. Common trade theretofore had been mostly in barter. Windham bank notes were a curiosity, and the $2 bills with their photographs of Col. Dyer and Col. Elderkin at either end, and the picture of fighting frogs in the centre, were the town's pride.

In 1854 the Windham Bank had been robbed of $7,000 in specie, and $15,000 in securities, the cashier, James Parsons, being bound and gagged. The watch dog was killed. Parsons quickly recovered himself and gave the alarm. The robbers then took a hand car at what is now Camp crossing, went to Norwich and hid in the woods on the Preston side. They were captured on a steamer when leaving Allyn's Point and most of the money was recovered. The robbers were sent to Wethersfield. The affair caused the biggest scare in Windham since the Frog fright.

In 1879, the old bank yielded to the popular pressure and was removed to Willimantic, where to-day it takes rank as a leading financial institution. Other banks have been organized in Willimantic, the Merchants' Loan and Trust in 1870, the Dime Savings Bank in 1872, the First National in 1878.

The Windham Centre of to-day remains a residence district, with not a few of her honorable old families remaining. In recent years she has caught a new life from the receding tide of the congested cities, and to-day the Green is growing in popularity as a summer resort, offering delightful opportunities for health and recreation. Handsome new trees, set by forethoughtful citizens a score of years ago, to succeed the ancient elms, have now grown to handsome proportions. The crumbling relics of ancient industries have been cleared away and modern Windham Green has donned a dress becoming to her new destiny. There is beginning a wholesome movement from the city to the town. We are learning that this huddling of people into cities is a mistake, and it is to be hoped that in the near future the land may be more evenly populated and more intelligently used. In such a development, Old Windham will share as well as the New.

LANDMARKS IN WILLIMANTIC.

There are at least five dwelling houses now standing in Willimantic borough which date back into the century preceding this. Two of them, the Hardin Fitch place at the west end, the old Josiah Dean (now called Cranston's) place at the east end on South Main street, are rivals for the claim of the oldest house in town, and date back at least two centuries. The other three are the Alfred Youngs (now Charles Young) place at the corner of South and Pleasant streets, the Waldo Cary (late John Smith's) place on Ash street by the North Windham road, and the Scott Smith place, corner of Brook and Main streets.

There is a noteworthy absence of business houses that have preserved their identity from the earliest days. There is no firm name in the borough now that was here in the beginning, except that of the Windham Manufacturing Company. Frank Wilson's drug store has been at the same stand since started in 1828, but with changing names. Thomas R. Congdon is the man who has been longest in business and is in actual trade to-day, with the Carpenter Bros. of West Main street as close followers. J. C. Bassett, John G. Keigwin, Turner and Wilson have long records but they have retired.

The most striking figure of the older parts of the town is the venerable Charles Smith of South Windham, a pioneer in the great industry of Smith, Winchester and Co., and now in his 80th year. He is yet in active business, and keeps in line with current events. He has been a man of marvelous energy, indomitable will, unflinching courage, sterling integrity and strong public spirit. His heart was shown in the small-pox scourge of 1874, when he fearlessly helped his suffering neighbors and saw that Willimantic was protected.

The most interesting figure on Willimantic streets is

General Lloyd E. Baldwin, now in his 82nd year. Born in Norwich in 1810, he removed to Mansfield, and as a boy he learned the builders trade in Willimantic, working on the Windham Co.'s "new mill" in 1828 and '29. In 1831 he set up in business for himself in Willimantic, and became the leading builder of early Willimantic. Among the buildings put up by him were the old Franklin Hall. Willimantic's first public building; also Joshua Lord's, Dr. Witter's, Elisha Williams's and Col. William L. Jillson's residences; the Linen Co.'s No. 3 mill, the Smithville Co.'s mill and three of their large dwelling houses, and a large share of the dwelling houses that stood in Willimantic in 1850. He also built churches at Danielsonville, Bozrah, Westchester, West Granby, Haddam, West Suffield, South Coventry and the old Broadway church in Norwich, also the first railway stations at Andover, Bolton, Vernon and Manchester; the first district school-house, center building of the present group. No man had more to do with the building of early Willimantic. He was postmaster here in 1843, and took the responsibility of moving the office uptown. He was a prominent figure in the old State Militia, and in politics in the '40s and '50s. He was colonel of the Fifth regiment and at one time general of the Fifth brigade, comprising the militia of Windham, Tolland and part of New London counties. He was candidate for state comptroller for three years, and member of the McClellan convention of '64, and candidate for presidential elector on the Seymour ticket of '68. He once served as escort for Andrew Jackson, marching across Norwich by his side, and he has remained to this day a staunch Democrat of the Jacksonian order, whom modern degeneracies cannot swerve from the strong faith of the fathers. He retains remarkable vigor and memory, and is daily seen on our streets, taking a lively interest in affairs.

Ex-Postmaster John Brown, long known as the "Republican War-horse," is another familiar figure. A sterling old patriot, his stirring words were wont to rouse the highest enthusiasm at public gatherings. He was a favorite moderator at town meetings for many years. For thirty-one years he has been connected with the post office, twelve years as Postmaster, and he still serves the public there.

One of the most significant and valuable of modern landmarks is the handsome iron fence that surrounds the Willimantic cemetery, the loving gift of George H. Chase of Stamford to the town that gave him birth, and in memory of his boyhood days at the old Laban Chase homestead. The spirit that prompted such a substantial gift was noble, and Windham owes him a lasting debt of gratitude.

I have discovered one instance of the continuance of the same occupation from generation to generation, in the same family, which is quite noteworthy and perhaps not parelleled in the town. In the early '30s William Tew, a venerable blacksmith, came from Rhode Island to Willimantic and occupied the large white house now standing on the southeast corner of Hooper's Lane (Winter street.) The old gentleman did not engage in blacksmithing here, but his son William did. William's son John is now the veteran blacksmith of the Willimantic of to-day, and John's son James is following the same honorable trade on Bank street. Robert Brown tells me that he has had horses shod by three generations of Tews, and hale and hearty at 70 he is waiting for a son of James to grow up and give him a fourth generation's shoeing. But Jim's only boy is thus far a girl, and Mr. Brown is getting a little discouraged. I have learned, however, that there is a woman in Worcester who shoes horses, and as women have already entered 4000 different occupations, horseshoeing may become as popular as type-writing, so that Mr. Brown must be patient and meanwhile Jim may be blessed with a boy!

WILLIMANTIC NEWSPAPERS.

The Windham "Herald" flourishing in Old Windham a century ago, fell into decline with the disintegration of the old town, and in 1820, Henry Webb began to publish in Brooklyn "The Independent Observer and County Advertiser." It was a larger paper than "The Herald," and was of course now published at the county seat. So "The Herald" succumbed. Later the Saturday "Transcript" of Killingly issued a Willimantic edition, and was finally established at Willimantic by John Collins, who carried it on until John Evans came here from Plattsburg, N. Y., with his brothers Charles and Edward, and bought "The Transcript," and established in its stead "The Public Medium," copies of which are still in existence, the headline bearing pictures of early Willimantic. "The Public Medium" was published every Saturday except when there were 53 weeks in the year, but suspended every 53rd week, we are told.

John Evans sold out to C. S. Simpson, a printer, who changed the name to Willimantic "Journal." Simpson did not succeed, however, and "The Journal" was suspended for a short time in 1861. Finally Evans took it back, and with William L. Weaver renewed its publication. Mr. Weaver built the paper to a high grade of character and influence, and made it distinguished by the historical and genealogical sketches which he published. He put into pamphlet form a portion of his genealogical researches and left many valuable documents which his son, Thomas Snell Weaver, by strange and happy fate, occupying to-day the same editorial chair, is making most admirable use of, to great public advantage. On Mr. Weaver's death in 1866, "The Journal" passed successively to Asa Curtis, Walt Pierson and W. J. Barber and in 1871 the late Henry L. Hall, son of Horace, and brother of Judge John M. Hall, became the editor, and continued for many years. His natural adaptation for the work was unsurpassed. He was Willimantic born and bred, his mind was keen, witty and appreciative, he was a natural orator of marked power, and a genial soul withal, and his career as editor of "The Journal," which he made one of the best weekly papers in the state, will be long remembered. He died in 1887. Arthur I. Bill, who had entered the office as printer's "devil," grew to be the chief business life of the concern, and in 1884 The Hall & Bill Printing Company started on a prosperous career, as chief printers to the Linen Company and general jobbers. Frank E. Beach became editor of "The Journal," but bought the Southbridge "Journal," and then came Thomas Snell Weaver, who needs no introduction to the community.

The Willimantic weekly "Enterprise" was started in 1877, by N. W. Leavitt of Scotland with Fayette Safford as assistant. In 1879, John A. McDonald of Danielsonville, who had been in their employ as a printer, joined a partnership with Mr. Safford and, as McDonald & Safford, they have since conducted the Willimantic "Chronicle," which has grown to be a permanent feature of the town.

"The Connecticut Home," State Temperance newspaper and advocate of the Prohibition party, was started here in 1886 by Allen B. Lincoln; was in 1890 removed to Hartford and now by combination with the Worcester "Times," has become "The New England Home."

Daily papers are numerous in Willimantic. W. C. Crandall started the Willimantic daily "Record" in 1881, but it was short lived.

The Willimantic daily "News" lived a few months in 1887 with J. H. Foster of Middletown as editor, and then expired. F. H. Alford of the Middletown "Herald" began the publication of the Willimantic "Herald" in 1891, and "The Chronicle" soon followed with a daily edition. Both are now running, and are creditable local dailies, but the field seems hardly large enough for two, if for one, and the outcome is problematical.

NOTES OF INTEREST.

An index of the growth of land values in later Willimantic may be seen in the fact that what was known as the Johnson Park property, including not only the square between North, Meadow, Bank and Valley streets, but the lot where A. G. Turner's silk mill now stands, and the land under the row of tenements on the South side of Meadow street, was all sold in 1863 for $1300. Recent sales from the same property show the market value of the same land to-day to be not less than $40,000.

The life of Dr. William Witter, first resident physician of Willimantic, and who lived in what is still known as the Witter house, on the east side of High street, corner of Main, was shortened by accident. When crossing the old bridge near the Stutely Sweet place in Coventry one day, the doctor's horse shied at a big stone in the road, and backed off into the river bed, gig, horse and man. Dr. Witter was seriously injured about the back.

He sued the town of Coventry and got a verdict for $1400. He always suffered from internal injuries after that, and though before the accident he bade fair to exceed fourscore and ten, he died at 44. Dr. Witter was called one of the best surgeons of his day east of the Connecticut River. When he first started here he charged his patients twenty-five cents a visit.

The Windham Center of about 1790-1820 was a great place for law students. Judge Hovey studied there. Judge Swift wrote his famous "Digest" there.

During the War of 1812, Charles Taintor, general tradesman at the Green, bought large quantities of provisions for the government to supply the soldiers, and this gave the Windham farmers quite a boom.

Warren Atwood bought the old Stanniford Inn, took it down and used it in some of his buildings in Willimantic, but I do not learn where.

William C. Cargell of Willimantic has in his possession a pig-weed cane which was growing in the sod by the old M. E. church where ground was broken for the Atwood Block. It is a curiosity.

James Walden was the first Adams Express Agent here in 1855 and used to carry most of the packages to the depot in his arms, or with a wheel-barrow. Now, teams are run, six men are employed all the time, and the gross receipts for the business average $125 a day.

One of the most active and energetic of Willimantic pioneers was Daniel Sessions who lived about two miles west of the village on the Coventry turnpike. Almost all the brick used in the late '20s and early '30s were made by him.

Young people will be interested to know that seventy-five years ago it was necessary for the young men and maidens who became engaged to have their bans published from the pulpit before they could be united in the holy estate of matrimony. It was generally done the Sunday before the great event.

Windham had some old slaves who were familiar figures down to 1840 or later. "Old Prime Dyer" has been immortalized with the frogs in Leavitt's operetta. There were also his sister "Cindy," another veteran negress called "Case Knife," and "Old Cruse White," who used to bleach hats and bonnets for the ladies. "Pete Smith" was another familiar figure. There were a score or more in town who remained here until death, employed in various capacities chiefly as field hands or domestics. Slavery was finally abolished in Connecticut in 1848.

A noteworthy attempt was made to start a shoe industry at Windham Center about forty years ago. Captain Justin Swift was President, and the capital subscribed was $10,000. The old shop, still standing next below the Parsons house, was built for the purpose, and about twenty hands were employed. Shoes were made and shipped to New York. Ten per cent dividends were soon declared and all went swimmingly for a time, but hard times came, extended credit was given to the New York commission house which sold the goods, and ere long the company awakened to the fact that most of its capital was in New York. Negotiations followed and the settlement was such that the industry was abandoned.

Windham has had three Congressmen under the new

constitution: John Baldwin, 1825-29, George S. Catlin, '43-45 and Alfred A. Burnham, '59-63. Baldwin was a Federalist of liberal tendencies; Catlin a Democrat of brilliant qualities who committed political suicide by voting for the admission of Texas; and Burnham a loyal Republican of war times, a gentleman of high moral character and marked ability, who also served as lieutenant-governor.

Henry Hall, brother of Horace, was first postmaster of Willimantic, establishing the office here in 1827. As he was clerk at the Windham Co.'s store, he located the office at the Hebard tavern, in charge of a deputy. George W. Hebard succeeded him and located the office at the Jillson stone store, opposite what is now the spool shop. Then came Col. Roswell Moulton who took it down to a building near by Edward F. Casey's present furniture store. In 1843 Gen. L. E. Baldwin became postmaster, and was audacious enough to locate the office uptown in a small building opposite Niles Potter's hotel (now Young's). Then came successively Joshua B. Lord in the Hanover Block, William L. Weaver at his store in Franklin building, James H. Work in the Twin buildings, Thomas Campbell in the Boon (now Card) block, then William H. Hosmer in the same place.

In 1861 James Walden was appointed and he held the office for eight years, locating it in his block on Main street, where now A. B. Williams's dry goods store is. John Brown followed for twelve years, then James Walden another term, then Henry N. Wales, and the present incumbent, Charles N. Daniels. The post office was removed by Postmaster Daniels in 1890 to the new Loomer block on North street, just back of the opera house. Mr. Brown remains as clerk, and has served in the office continuously for thirty-one years.

In '49, when the California gold fever broke out, Windham furnished three men for the company that sailed from New London: Allen Stoddard, William Webb and Mosely Curtis.

OUR PRESENT POPULATION.

A word about our present population will be timely. Of the 10,000 in town (8,600 being in the borough) not far from 2,300 are of Irish extraction, about 1,800 of French Canadian extraction, and nearly all the remainder of English origin. There are about 300 Swedes and 50 colored persons. Of the first named, only about 600 were born in Ireland, the rest are native Americans. The Canadians have not been as long among us, but they are a rapidly growing people, and the proportion of foreign born among them is fast decreasing.

Irishmen first appeared in Willimantic in considerable numbers about 1840 to work for Jillson and Capen. They were as much of a curiosity to our people, as we to them, and at least as awkward as we should be in Ireland. Irish blunders, coupled with native Irish wit, supplied the almanacs with jokes for a generation. They came in large numbers to help build the railroads, and then to enter the mills. From the first they have come to stay, practically an English speaking people, or at least with no adherence to their native tongue, for I have yet to learn of an Irish immigrant parent who has transmitted his language to his American-born children. The Irish came here, driven from oppression to freedom, to find a home, and to become Americans. They have never shown any tendency to return. They are intelligent and thrifty, as modern Willimantic is showing. To-day their share of the taxable grand list is over $300,000; they are building many homes, and they are as much attached to this country as any of its inhabitants. Thirty graves of sacred memory in the Catholic cemetery testify to their loyalty to the old flag in 1861. To show how rapidly they are becoming indigenous to our soil, we have only to recall that the census of 1860 showed 490 born in Ireland, while to-day with our population tripled, the Irish born scarcely exceed 600. I saw a photograph group of young Irish-Americans of Willimantic, a few days ago, and they looked more American than Irish.

With the Canadians it was different at the outset. They came here about 1852 to work in the Smithville mills and they had no purpose to stay, but thought to accumulate wages and return to Canada. Their national ties were much stronger than those of the Irish and they took care to preserve their language and teach it to their children. But the public schools and the American ideas are doing their inevitable work. The Frenchmen, too, are learning to love Willimantic, and in later years have been less and less inclined to leave it. Their little self-owned homes are scattered here and there, and the tax-list now rates their taxable property at $60,000, almost entirely in little buildings which bespeak volumes of interest in the new and with many of them native land. Irish immigration has practically ceased, but Canadians are still coming. Both classes multiply more rapidly than does the older native stock. Together they make up to-day nearly half of our population. They have as much right here as any one, and they are as well disposed. We welcome them. The historic ties of Ireland, France and America are peculiarly kindred in the struggle for liberty.

THE FUTURE.

To-day we stand face to face with the Windham of the future. What shall it be? It may be great. We have within our borders the making of a large and prosperous city of wholesome character. How can it be done?

The first thing we need is *public spirit*, a better realization of the principle that the good of the least, is the good of all.

We need more loyalty and confidence in our own town, and in each other;—less of this pulling and hauling by rings and cliques for selfish ends, and more of united action for the general welfare, which is always the best welfare of each; less of that spirit which looks upon every new industry as a rival, and chokes off every projected improvement which does not benefit "my property." We need less of that financial short-sightedness that will stake its all on a Wall street margin or chase an imaginary ten-per-cent dividend into a silverless Montana earth-pit, and more of that practical common sense which knows that earnings reinvested in our own town at four per cent will promote a growth that in a few years will add another four per cent, with the further advantage of knowing where your property is!

We need better unity in education. It is time we abolished the hap-hazard school-district system and adopted an intelligent educational policy. The state offers us superior advantages, and we should hasten to improve them. And as for the public school, the one great fact for us all to realize is, that whatever our origin or nationality, one, two, three, or a dozen generations back, and whatever our personal religious creed, the one hope for an harmonious future is in a common education in a common school, and the development of our children into an homogeneous people. This is true of Town, State and Nation, and I am particularly pleased to add that, by inquiry, I find it to be the common sentiment of the more intelligent representatives of the three nationalities of which we are chiefly composed.

We need a better understanding and appreciation of each other. The problem of the nation is represented in Willimantic. We must look less to the accident or environment of birth and more to the character and spirit of the man. We are here together to stay. Our interests are common, not diverse, and we must seek to develop our agreements, not our differences.

We need a keener sense of what the public welfare demands, and courage to follow it. We need to recognize that right principles are the product of experience, and that right action has a positive, practical value as well as an eternal moral obligation.

Loyalty to Windham, loyalty to each other, loyalty to conscience, is the spirit in which we shall face the future, and so through the third century of our beloved community, may God speed the right!

THE EPIC OF WINDHAM.

[BY THERON BROWN.]

One day of the days divine,
  When the gods roamed everywhere,
The horse of the sacred Nine
  Came down from his path in the air;
His lightning hoof fell first
  On the slope of Helicon green,
And out of that footprint burst
  The fountain of Hippocrene.

And ever since then the thought
  Of the world the story has kept,
And scholar and sage have sought
  The place where Pegasus stepped;
And the hole of the white hoof still
  O'erflows with the magic spring
Where the poets drink their fill
  And the daughters of music sing.

Will the fountain's flow ever cease?
  Will the old tale ever die out?
Its part in the fame of Greece
  Do any deny or doubt?
Do you call the dreamer a dolt
  Whose fancy and faith indorse
The myth of Minerva's colt,
  The Muses' family horse?

From the humblest ground that shows
  The dent of the flying steed
Some slip of poetry grows,
  Some flower of immortal seed.
Full many a hamlet's pride,
  Full many a city's seal
Is the stamp where Pegasus tried
  The weight of his wizard heel.

One night, on the rising whiff
   Of the wind of a new renown,
The wonderful hippogriff
   Came sailing o'er Windham town.
Swift Hill just under his girth
   Rose green, but he went beyond,
And his hind foot struck the earth
   At the bottom of Follett's Pond.

The village woke at the whack.
   Had they heard a cannon explode?
Ten to one on the stallion's back
   That night Bellerophon rode.
For the noise that followed him roared
   With a terrible warlike din
As if all Waterloo poured
   From the hole that the horse broke in.

In the ballads early and late
   Still echoes the hullaballoo
From seventeen fifty and eight
   To eighteen ninety and two.
And the fame of that battle dark
   Will sing over Windham Green
Till the last frog ceases to bark
   In the mud of her Hippocrene.

The maps of glory make room
   For the town with a tale to tell;
You are sure of a world-wide boom
   Where the Muses open a well.
And to stir a song from its source
   In the dirt of the prosy trades
One kick of the wingèd horse
   Is better than forty spades.

The silent ballads of the tawny tribes
Will never sound again. No warrior scribes
Compiled on strip or scroll the tuneful spoil
Of the wild ancients of our homestead soil.
No word of savage minstrel points to-day
To where their Tempès and Arcadias lay,
Nor lives one leaf or line of lettered lore,
By hand of feathered priest or sagamore,
To tell a rescued region's paler sons
The story of her earliest Marathons.

WINDHAM BANK, ERECTED 1832, ON COURT HOUSE SITE.

Barbarian fate! Those first New England men
Who plucked the eagles—never made a pen.
Their gaudy helmets tossed the inkless quills;
Their arrows strewed them on these heedless hills,
And left their speech, their thought, their life, their age,
A glimmering legend on an empty page.

But o'er their fields by peaceful white men plowed
Break the same wind and thunder from the cloud,
Fall the same dew, and rain, and snow, and sleet,
That wet, in strife or chase, their buskined feet,
In the same tones through summer, winter, spring,
The Willimantic and Shetucket sing,
The same sun shines, the stars unsleeping glow
Out of the dim colonial long ago,
While here and there some local memory frames
The forest music of the red men's names,
And curious fancy, half unriddling, reads
Their "totems" on our queer ancestral deeds.

Between the shadowy days of Nipmuck land
New-conquered by the fierce Mohegan's hand,
When Joshua Attawanhood, with his dog
Hunted on Brick-top, angled in Natchaug,
Or in his wigwam carved his powder horn
While Sowgonask, his Podunk squaw, hoed corn,—
Between those days (whose echoes still ascend
From Millard's Meadow to Hop River Bend,)
And the first planting of a Christian home,
The ghosts of Andros and King Philip came
To tell how meanly, by their marplot aid,
This bi-centennial was ten years delayed.
But we forgive them. Their ungracious part
Assured and strengthened our historic start,
And gave us a "first-settler" to engage
The careless eyes that skip our title page.

Late in the seventeenth century's afternoon,
Unlike the moon-man, who "came down too soon,"
Our Englishman *from* Norwich found his way
Up where these meadows in the sunshine lay,
And, forced to exile by some strange renown,
Became the Cecrops of a Yankee town.
    Mysterious foreigner! still silent waits
The story of van-courier John Cates.
A wandering star untraced by friends or foes,

Men saw him set who knew not where he rose.
Romantic fancy, hovering where he died,

Ranked him "lieutenant," called him "regicide,"
Marked him red-handed from the Cromwell wars,
Pious and pitiless, and at our doors
In fable now the British bull-dog snarls
For the stray Roundhead who helped kill King Charles.
Pious he was, and Puritan, possessed
Of worldly goods, a gentleman, a guest
Of Pilgrim Land, a friend of high and low,
A freeman—and he owned a slave, black Joe!

Enough that by the moral light he saw,
When liberty was only white men's law,
His human chattel was no swift reproof
To one whose soul had felt oppression's hoof,
Since Right, to even a Mayflower refugee,
Implied no negro's title to be free.

We trust the legend that John Cates was kind,
As kind of heart as liberal of mind,
And, after twice four years of upright deeds,
And generous thoughts for Windham's future needs,
When, praised for scattered blessings, he who gave
The town's first dwelling filled its earliest grave,
That the green threshold of his churchyard inn
Was watered by the tears of black Joe Binn.

Round that first farmstead, settling one by one,
New households gathered; Windham was begun.
Along old "Nipmuck path" her street was laid,
And peace built mansions where barbarians played.
Survey, through Time's inverted glass again
That corporation of eleven men.
One less than Israel's chiefs, the chosen few
Numbered in mid-May, sixteen-ninety-two,
At the same figure where, in hopeful doubt,
Th' apostles stood—with Judas' name left out.
They had no use for Judas in their plan,
Those honest souls, united man to man.
Their law of living from one book they learned,
In all their seven houses altars burned.
They kept the Sabbath day, they never swore,
And, with the horseshoe hung o'er every door,
They balked the devil, and the Salem fad
That drove, that year, all Massachusetts mad.

They thrived—and if with one good-natured lift
"Luck in odd numbers" helped their infant thrift
Their earliest parson kept the fact in mind,
Who served the town, in good old Bradford kind,
With olive branches, frequent, fresh and green,
And never stopped until he raised thirteen!
And all that baker's dozen did so well
That to this day the Whitings "wear the bell."

'Twas with a saintly vision, sorrow-free
Our fathers faced th' uncertain yet-to-be.
They fed their herds and tilled their virgin farms,
They felled the forests with their sturdy arms,
They drove to Norwich wharf their brindled teams
With hay, and grain, and pine and hemlock beams,
And piles of cheese, and barrelled beef and pork,
And bales of home-knit stockings for New York,
They counted eggs, and measured meal and milk,
They weighed wool fleeces, while their wives made silk,
They shared their plenty in Thanksgiving joys,
They schooled and catechised their girls and boys,
They met at Goodman More's to sing and pray,
They praised their preacher's work—with solid pay—
The Levite portion in their parted grounds,
Good corn, good wood, good meat and sterling pounds,
Nor ever dreamed, in simple faith secure,
That calm, idyllic life would not endure.

New neighbors came; apace the hamlet grew;
O'er vacant lots the building fever flew,
Till the swift orders fairly put to pain
Jonathan Jennings with his saw and plane.
Soon rose the meeting-house, the church was born,
Soon rose the mills, for lumber and for corn.
No prophet then saw Windham stretch her neck
Up Willimantic to Naubeseteck
To read her fortune in the river-gorge
On the wild rocks by Daniel Badger's forge.
Nor when, next century, like Elijah's cloud,
John Cates's handful had become a crowd,
Could the grave fathers own without a pang
The noisier tune old "Southeast Quarter" sang.
The psalmist's "sparrow" fretted on its perch ;
Faith took new forms, each precinct had its church.
Austere dissensions vexed the gospel-fold,
Debate grew hot, and piety grew cold.

Came mortal sickness next, and where it swept
In half the village homes some mother wept,
And strong men fell, and pastors on their knees
Said prayers for them, and died—then thro' the trees
"A sound of going," like King David's sign
To meet the midnight foes of Palestine,
Stirred the unwilling souls that waited for
The threatened terrors of a border war.
'Twas in that weak, unsettled, sad, half-blind,
Foreboding, wishful, timorous state of mind
Our fathers heard another sound, whose fame,
In mirth immortal linked to Windham's name,
Has laughed to health more hypochondriacs
Than ever convalesced on Holmes or Saxe.
O'er half the globe the very nurseries learn
The swampy music of that droll nocturne.
In pamphlets, scrap books from collectors' shears,
In histories, cyclopedias, gazetteers,
Song-books and school-books—where the English tongue
Is talked or read—the tale is said or sung.
We tell it gladly, smiling with the rest
To think how far its fun the world has blessed,
And rail at Parson Peters in our pride
No more—but O, how Parson Peters lied!

In the periwig times of old Governor Fitch—
Fifty-four, Fifty-eight, call it either or which—
In seventeen-hundred-and-something-half-way,
At the close of a sweltering midsummer day,
By the East Windham grist mill, a mile out of town,
The flood-gate was up and the water was down;
For the owner or miller—Job, Peter or Sam,
Had drawn off the pond while he tinkered the dam;
And the bull-frogs that peopled the mud-puddle gloom
Rubbed heads in the shallows and crowded for room.
Each croaker, beginning his first serenade,
Felt a haul and a hitch in the music he made,
And elbowed his fellows with croupy complaint,
Till the humor of all took the quarrelsome taint,
And missing the seat where he commonly sung,
Every Punch had a crack in his temper and lung.
"Cudderow, cudderow," grumbled little and great;
"You plug," said old Pop-eye. "You plague," said his mate;
"Jug o' rum," thundered Yellow throat; "Slum," echoed back,
The meanest and wartiest sneak in the pack.
The concert was broken; they tried it in vain;

The low-water tangle was symphony's bane.
Once more, and once more they began it, but no ;
They could pitch the old notes, but the chime wouldn't go.
The hole in the milldam had narrowed their brink,
And stinted their song when it stinted their drink,
And the mischief had put the whole pond out of tune
On that moonless and starless old evening in June.
   So it went, till at midnight the jangle of sound
Broke loose like a Bedlam shot out of the ground.
Had the demon of discord who fingered the dice
In the Homeric war of the frogs and the mice
Whispered "rats" down the stream thro' the Windhamite fens
And fooled the bog-jumpers to fight their own friends?
Was it witchcraft? Be sure had it happened before
By summers and winters some three and three score,
'Twere the toss of a copper some crazy old dame
Would have died for the rumpus—or shouldered the blame.
No, the romantic theory patented last
Brings never a broomstick a-whisk on the blast,
But calls all the gods of Parnassus to say
The colt of Minerva that night got away
And found that just here, at the critical time,
He had put "his foot in it," and started a rhyme,
And stirred up the angry batrachian Mars
To an uproar that frightened him back to the stars.
   Go down on the old Scotland turnpike, and guess
The rage and the ramp of that web-footed mess
And the blatant alarm in our forefathers' ears
That could echo a hundred and thirty-eight years.
All the frogs in the fables ran never so mad
As the tribe in that basin that went to the bad
When the touch of a vagabond sprite set afire
Every cold-blooded liver that grew in the mire.
A thousand blind furies in bottle-green coats
Fell afoul with a howl and a clutching of throats,
And the battle waxed hot, and the swell of the storm
Swept in every reptile that croaked in the swarm,
Till the whole slimy kindred of Jack-in-the-pool
Were twisted and mixed like a mackerel school
In a slippery, squirming, unspeakable hash
Of lunatic frenzy to strangle and smash.
There was Blunderhead crushing poor Peep like an egg,
There was Drum-Billy butting young Grasshopper-leg,
There were Humpback and Cottonmouth, Shiney and Stripe,
Hee-haw, Wallow-swallow, Bim-bome, Little-pipe,
Thorough-bass, Ganderfoot, Wapperjaw, Doubledone,

And Bulldoze, and Speckle, and Son-of-a-gun,
And Tom-in-the-cattails, and Crocodile-rib,
And giant Swamp-cabbage, and dwarf Yellow-bib,
And Longshank, and Polly-wog, White-eye, and Turk,
And Dog-face, and Loafer-that-watches-the-work,
Peagreen, Silver-Dude, Monkey-nose, and Dull-thud,
And Bawler, and Sprawler, and Stick-in-the-mud,
And fat Beetle-dragon, and slim Hammer-tongue,
And Quack, and Fog-trumpet, and Chop, and Cow-lung,
Go-bang, Bellows-bag, Shovel-lip, Thunder-bug,
And Wheezer, and Sneezer, and Honker and Chug,
And Squatter, and Squealer, and Brag, and Bow-wow,
All mixed in the tussle, and booming the row.
    They kicked, and they splashed, and they spattered and swore, '
They wrestled and tumbled all over the shore :
There were scrapings and scratchings without any claws,
There were biters that hadn't a tooth in their jaws,
There were chokings and pinchings nobody could see,
And death to the undermost wretch in the spree.
The mill-water smoked like a buffalo-drive,
The midnight, the darkness itself seemed alive.
The black hurly burly shot horrible sounds
Like the Wild Hunter's bugle and bellowing hounds,
Or the Walpurgis revel that suddenly starts
At the bidding of fiends in the glens of the Hartz;
And the trick of the air made them gather and go
To the westward, away from the valley below
So high that the miller-folk, seasoned to all
The dogs on the turnpike and cats on the wall,
Lay still while the frogs clamored hither and yon,
And let the uncouth bombilation go on,
Tho' it jarred every bedstead and window and door
As if a small earthquake rolled under the floor.
But the roar on the east wind, that went to the town,
No charm could break up and no reason sleep down.
It tore thro' the heart of the mid-summer calm,
And shook all the clouds over Joshua's farm.
Every bird on its roost felt the rush of the rout,
Every leaf on the dew-dabbled trees was a shout,
Every cubical inch of the shivering mist
Held an ounce of blue thunder that hit like a fist,
And, alas, for the house that was shingled too thin
When the dream-breaking din-devil knocked to come in!
    The first human soul in the village awake
Was a poor rattled negro—the minister's Jake—

Who ran thro' the streets at a hurricane pace
With a budget of tidings as black as his face,
And howled at the windows on Meeting-house Square,
"Dar's sumfin' a happenin' up in the air!"
What is it? The sleepers pick open their eyes;
Every hair of their heads is a creeping surprise.
The pillows are empty before the cock-crow:
It has come—Windham's historic moment of woe!
In night-caps and slumber-gowns, barefoot and pale,
The people stand helpless, like weeds in a gale.
From the roar of the Babel which way will they fly?
They huddle, they shudder, they whisper, they cry,
With hearts that stop beating, and faces that blench
"Prepare for the Indians! Look out for the French!
There's a tomahawk dance, and a battle refrain!
The powows are out, over on Chewink Plain!"
They listen; the clamor grows heavy and grum—
The tramp of an army! the throb of the drum!
Till the sound's very fury the notion destroys;
Would a foe that was "stealing a march" make a noise?
Some terror more solemn than war must be nigh:
'Twas the trump of the Judgment, the wreck of the sky!

    Ah, sufferers smitten with sense of their blames!
Some fancied strange voices repeating their names.
Grave town-folk of local and civil repute,
Plain yeomen, sharp tradesmen, stood ghastly and mute,
And lawyers, and doctors, and deacons, appalled,
Wondered how came the summons, and why they were called;
And loudest of all in the frightful ado
Rang up "Col. Dyer!" and "Elderkin too!"
    What said the stout Colonel now sleeps in his grave.
But the thought of poor Cuffee, his gray-headed slave,
When he caught the wild note of the ending of Time,
Came out like a victor-cry, quaintly sublime,
"I'm glad on't, I be! I'm glad on't, I be!
My hard work is ober—dis niggah is free!"
There were wailings of children afraid of their lives,
There were shriekings and swoonings of mothers and wives
There were shakings of strong men, and pallors of dread,
And rash words, forgotten the hour they were said,
There was mounting in haste by the bravest (they say
The horsemen were Elderkin, Dyer, and Gray),
And they rode with a watch, and they rode with a will
Straight out of the village and up Mullein Hill,—
Then silently back, with a sting in their ears,
And a smile for the women and children in tears,—

And the sounds in the sky grew less awful and loud
When a curt explanation had scattered the crowd,
Till the hubbub and horror died where they were born,
And the scare of the midnight left shame for the morn.

But the cry of poor Cuffee, wrung out of a breast
That never knew Liberty's blessing of rest,
As it spoke thro' the tumult of doom in the air
The pathos of triumph in spite of despair,
Still lives in the lore of that wonderful fright,
To challenge a world that denied him his right,
And tells of the patience its burden that bore
So long without hope it could dread nothing more.
Could the pity of heaven, that counted his tears,
Have lengthened and strengthed his life thirty years,
Till the Blue-law dominion turned white in the sun
That shone on her freedom when justice was done,
The simple old slave in his happy surprise
Would have known that God's angel, tho' slowly he flies,
May come to the help of His mourners, and say
Some great benedictions before the Last Day.
But he knew it when death on his ebony brow
Put his crown, and he knows it in jubilee now,
While Peace o'er his ashes, in blossoming turf,
Writes "king" on the ground where he toiled as a serf,
And her benison falls, like a leaf from a tree,
"His hard work is over, the bondman is free."

When the morning was bright and the water was still
The good Windham fathers went down to the mill,
Where, in white-bellied ruin turned up to the day,
The last that was left of the mystery lay.
'Twas a mystery still. Of the hundreds they found
On the battle-field slain not a frog had a wound !
And whether they worried themselves out of breath
Or were strangled and bulldozed, and bellowed to death
Or squelched by the nightmare that rode in the fen,
Is as much of a riddle this moment as then ;
And the poets who rhyme the old story, and feign
A demigod's doing where none can explain,
May kill off the frogs with an epic or ode,
And leave the whole question to run in the road.

The sound of a harp built a city in Greece,
And Rome was once saved by the cackle of geese
Great London grew rich by a grasshopper's chat,
And her longest lord mayor was made by a cat.

As we come in the prime of our own ninety-two
To the scene of last century's June bugaboo,
Our meed to its memory measures its claim,
To the worth of all trifles that bloom into fame.
We'll grudge not a whit of its folly and fun
To the legend that gave us our marvellous run,
But leaving our rivals, who banter our prize,
To the fate of the dealer who don't advertise,
Like the church or the party that wears on its breast
The nickname its enemies gave it in jest,
We'll nail to our lintels the bullfrog burgee
Of the Windham that was for the Windham to be.

Another century;—and these pleasant fields,
Still rich with all the sweets that summer yields,
Asked of the streets, that made them no reply,
Where were the busy throngs that once passed by.
From Quinnebaug the cocks of Brooklyn crew,
"Keep the old court house and we'll keep the new."
And all the partridges of Pond-town beat
"Old Windham is no more the county seat."
The lonely mother took a last survey
O'er the broad freeholds she had given away,
Then saw, between her rivers narrowed down,
Her suburb more a city than a town,
And swift divining, as she viewed the scene,
The mammon mystery of her slighted Green,
Admired the thrifty paradox that planned
To swell her census while it shrank her land.
Enough that Fate's decree, and Plutus' will,
Emptied the farmhouse and o'erflowed the mill,
Her life was like the years that marked her walls,
Pure at the spring and wealthy at the Falls.
Old "Center," helpless in her lean extreme,
Must move, or die—or radiate up the stream.
She chose the last, to please the civil whim
That stints the heart to feed the biggest limb.
Her churches knocked at Willimantic doors;
Her offices, fire companies, and stores
Went the same way; the taverns marched in rank,
And last of all went Windham County Bank.

(I pause to nurse a quaint remembrance here,
That bank and I were born the self-same year.
I mind its notes, between whose figures poked
Two frogs—so lifelike that they almost croaked;
The original "greenbacks," of the native race,

That long anticipated Salmon Chase,
They blossomed, like pond lilies from the mud,
Memento of a war that shed no blood,
And proof how frugal wit a joke can seize
And turn to shrewd account the sorest tease.
That bank held my first pittance in its tills;
I went through college on those bull-frog bills;
And when my next ancestral check comes in
I'll get the cash from my old fiscal twin.)

Home of my sires, on thy historic clock,
Since Captain Abbee out of Norwich dock
Sailed the sloop Windham, with its pennon slim,
Its golden-lettered streak, its snowy trim,
Its green frog figurehead—and proudly bore
Thy modest commerce to Manhattan's shore,
Time's creeping hands have crossed the age of steam,
To where the lightnings of new noonday gleam,
And the *town* Windham, with her helm alee,
Swings into port, and rigs again for sea.
Fate, to this summit hour from long ago
Twice round the century-dial following slow,
Has left forever shining by the way
Some broken sunbeams of each faded day.
The light of old instruction will not fail
The church that gave a president to Yale;
Old patriotism haunts the place that bred
One of the Signers whom John Hancock led;
Old courage lives that burned in heroes' veins
Who, from this village, fought in four campaigns;
Old worth and wisdom in the garden wait
That raised a full-grown governor of the state;
The same old Word bears witness unimpeached,
Where stalwart Whiting and Devotion preached;
And if old basement thrift has climbed up stairs
God bless our wealth, and save our millionaires!

Our mother! backward to thy morning star
We scan the past that made us what we are.
Tell us, thy debtors, tell us, nurse of men,
What Windham-now can do for Windham-then.
Her ancient silence grows a vision seen—
There stands a cenotaph on yonder Green—
Its polished tablets rich with names and dates,
Its bust the ideal form of Founder Cates.
Recumbent round his shaft their living sons

Count his ten colleagues in eternal bronze;
Along the solid plinth, in cameo brown,
Brave scenes of civic story sketch the town,
While keen beholders, questioning below,
Spy the bent shapes of Cuffee and poor Joe,
And in one small cartouche, obscurer still,
The carved *fac simile* of a frog bank bill.

    Bucolic hamlet, if thy children say
Such monuments are money thrown away,
Bid them at least in sacred honor hold
The lingering remnants of thy life of old,
Preserve the pious hopes and pure desires
That fed and fanned her morning altar-fires,
And teach again thy first domestic lore
In modern homes where hearthstones glow no more.

    To thee, fair Centre, pilgrims, fain to greet
Thy busy borough clamoring at thy feet,
Soon tiring of its bustle and its throng,
When earth is bright and summer days are long,
Escape, where nature never hears or feels
The humming spindles and the roaring wheels.
Thy scene of leafy calm and breezy space
To us will every year be "Hither Place"
Until thy vanished saints in dream pass by
And call us to the Yonder Place on high.

AT HOME.

[BY JOSEPHINE M. ROBBINS.]

We come to-day with friendly hearts,
With cordial words and true,
To tender greetings from our town
To this old town and you.
We feel to-day as they may feel
Who to their own home band
Come back from other homes to clasp
Their dear ones by the hand.

We once were yours! Our little town
Was once of yours a part,
And side by side we walked with you,
Thought flew from heart to heart.
When tyranny upon the throne
Sought to lay freedom low,
Our sires with yours went forth to meet
And fight a foreign foe.

At Bowling Green one helped to pull
King George's statue down,
At sad Long Island's brave retreat
One marched with Washington
Close at his side, so near a hand
Might almost touch his cloak.
All night he marched in solemn tread,
No word the silence broke.

All through New Jersey's sharp campaign
Our soldier's camp fire burned
With Arnold, Durkee, Knowlton, till
The tide of war was turned.
A valiant son of worthy sire,
Who at his country's beck,
Went forth with gallant Wolfe, to aid
In the taking of Quebec.

Long years they've rested side by side
In the churchyard in the vale.
Three other names are there, brave hearts
Whose courage did not quail,
One starving on a war ship lay
Thro' months of weary pain,
Yet lived to see his friends and home
And little ones again.

In 1812 when British ships
As they had done before,
Threatened with faggot and with fire
The towns along the shore,
Our sires with yours went bravely forth
And quickly marching down
Saved, by their presence, from the torch,
The threatened harbor town.
When treason reared its hydra head
In freedom's darkest night,
Our men with yours went side by side,
To battle for the right.
God knoweth and man knows their deeds,
How bravely and how well
They bore the brunt of battle shock,
The pain of prison cell.

Our hopes, our joys, our interests
With yours are still the same,
If you do well we share with you
The glory and the fame.
We love to name when far from home,
Our *country* brave and true,
Old Windham County, dear to all,
Received its name from you.

Long as her rocky hills shall last,
Long as her rivers run,
The memory of her gallant deeds,
Her battles bravely won,
Shall dwell within her children's hearts,
Wherever they may roam,
And coming to Old Windham Green,
Be always coming home.

THE FIRST SETTLER.

[BY JANE GAY FULLER.]

Two hundred years ago, they say,
A homeless exile came this way,
In search of some secure retreat
For weary head and weary feet.
From colony to colony
The man had wandered; never free
From apprehension, and the dread
Of sovereign vengeance on his head;
For what offence we cannot tell,
As he preserved the secret well.

'Tis said he was a regicide,
Whose hands in royal blood were dyed;
It seems most probable, for then
The regicides were death-doomed men.
But little know we of this man,
Except he was a Puritan
Who rode with Cromwell side by side
And sang, "Let God be glorified,"

While hurling weapons at the foe;
For honest men will fight you know
For church and creed so long ago;
And toleration was not learned
While Quakers hung, and witches burned,
And good men thought to pleasure God
With whipping-post and scourging-rod.

In times like these our settler came,
And left behind him home and name;
He called himself John Cates, but we
Have never learned his pedigree.
It matters not; enough renown
To be the Father of our Town.

He was not poor; he had enough
Of worldly raiment, worldly stuff,
With gold and silver in his chest,
Brought from afar o'er land and wave
Nor was he Abolitionist,
For in the South he bought a slave,

A trusty servant, faithful friend,
Who loved his master to the end.
You all have heard of "Guinea Joe,"
Who would have been a settler, too,
If he had been a man, you know!

The forest welcomed him! The breeze
Brought back the tuneful melodies
His childhood loved beyond the seas!
And blue-birds sang, and blossoms sprang
To cheer the lonely-hearted man,
Till others came; then life began
Anew for the poor refugee
Unsought in his obscurity.

Two hundred years have passed away,
Years of progression and decay;
Old names have vanished, old renown;
But the first settler of our town
Will live in Windham history
While children learn their a-b-c,
And pious laymen and divine
Drinks from his cups the sacred wine.

We owe this man, for treasure lent
To church and school, a monument.
A debt of honor! Townsmen say—
"We'll guarantee that debt to-day!"

"THE TOWN OF SCOTLAND."

[RESPONSE BY EDWIN BAKER GAGER.]

Mr. Chairman, Ladies and Gentlemen:
When I received the invitation of your secretary to respond for the youngest of Old Windham's daughters, my native town of Scotland, I could do nothing else than comply. In form only was it a request. In spirit it was imperative. And I was in the position of the old Puritan believer in foreordination whom Dr. Twichell told of at the last New England dinner in New York. A certain thing had to be done by him which he much disliked to do, and he said, "I wouldn't do it if I didn't believe it had been foreordained from all eternity, and I've a good mind not to anyhow." I thought of the beautiful valley over beyond the eastern hills and the kindly spirit of the friends over there who joined with your secretary in asking me to answer for them, and here I am.

I have the youngest daughter of this venerable town to answer for and in this I am fortunate. The youngest daughter is always the favorite. If not exceeding large in territory or population nor very heavily loaded down with the material results which are the goal of this rushing, busy age, yet she is very fair to look upon, she has an indomitable spirit and is greatly beloved of her own; and in the turn of fickle Fortune's wheel we look for something which shall lift her out of her present material languishment and again adorn her with those jewels of which she has been temporarily stripped by the chance of industrial development.

CATES MEMORIAL TABLET AT WINDHAM CEMETERY.

If our town does not to-day occupy the relatively high position she held thirty or even a hundred years ago, if, like Hecuba, she sits alone mourning for her children who have gone, it is not because they are lost, but because she has lavished her strength upon other communities. In 1860 her population was something like one thousand, now it is less than five hundred. Would you find them? Go to Providence, to Norwich, to Hartford; go far west to Nebraska, where is an entire colony of Scotland people; go to Willimantic, come right to Windham, where you have chosen a Scotland boy for your secretary, and there are the thriving, energetic people who would still have been within our borders had it not been for the accident of railway location and the absence of water-power; there is the brawn and muscle and mental power which Scotland has produced.

From the migration to Wyoming, way back in our history, even to the present, we have sent out a stream of emigrants to other parts of this state and of the nation. As a town, we have cast our bread upon the waters and we hope and believe that after many days it will return, as it has already begun to do in many of our country towns, as it has begun to do, if I mistake not, here about this very Windham Green.

These epochal celebrations are well worth noting carefully. For all of us, youngest as well as oldest, it is "now or never." The "Elixir of Life" is still to be found, and one celebration like this is our limit. In this rushing, restless busy age, our gaze is so fixed upon the present and immediate future, that there is danger lest we lose our bearings, that we become intoxicated by the mad whirl of this era of steam and electricity. It is well, as we have done to-day, to take in our history at a single glance, to grasp it as a whole, to consider our small beginnings and the long and often arduous struggle of two hundred years through which "God hath brought us on our way." Such a survey tends to sober us up, to show us what a slow process this historical growth has been, and that we should not be too proud of the present, for when the quadricentennial of this old town is held, we with our celebration here to-day will seem quite as phantasmal, quite as quaint and unreal, as the few settlers who held the first meeting of this town in June, 1692, now seem to us. It is a good time to study up our local history, to bring back the dwellers in the ancient cemeteries of our towns and make the old times pass in panoramic view before us. This work has been done for us in the able sketches of Mr. Weaver and Mr. Lincoln. By them these two hundred years now gone have been made very real, and there is not one of us who has listened to these historical sketches, but has felt his love for Old Windham and for the parts of it which have set up for themselves revivified and strengthened.

Speaking for the inhabitants of Scotland and for myself, we are proud of the honorable history of Windham. We are proud too of the part we have played in the history of this town. We do not wonder that you did not wish us to go, or that you compelled us to serve seven, yes a dozen times seven years, before we got our freedom, and even then we went without a dowry. No, not quite without, for our history for a hundred and fifty years, though written with that of Windham, was after all our own. And as I listen to Windham's story and the part our town has played in it, as I read of the Devotions and Waldos, and Kingsleys, and Robinsons, and Carys, and Palmers, and Basses, and Huntingtons, of the Webbs, and Burnhams, and Tracys, and Fullers, and many more I might name, descendants of the Huguenot and Scotch Presbyterian settlers, I thank the kind Providence which led these men to follow the lead of the Scotchman, Isaac Magoon, and pitch their tents in the charming valley named from the most picturesque and charming portion of the British Isles.

When we who have gone out from this old, new town think on these things, surely we feel our hearts within us burn, we think fondly of the memories of our early days spent upon its rugged hillsides and in its pleasant valleys, we search to the ends of the earth to find the whereabouts of our early companions, lovingly and reverently we think of our kindred sleeping their last sleep in its bosom, and for those who remain to guard the ancient firesides, we say, God be with you. Make you keep the altar fires of these old families burning, may you live to see our town take a new lease of life, when it shall again become what it was a century ago, an intellectual and a social center for the communities round about.

"THE YOUNGER GENERATION."

[RESPONSE BY AMOS LAWRENCE HATHEWAY.]

Mr. President, Ladies and Gentlemen:—

In rising so late, and after so ample a literary feast as we have had to-day, I am reminded of the story of the after-dinner orator who responded to a toast very late in the evening. "At this late hour," said he, in a voice full of yearning, "after so full a measure of rhyme and reason has been meted out to you, what can I say to you—what shall I talk about?" And the unexpected response came promptly from a wearied patriot at the foot of the table—"Talk about a minute!" I can almost fancy that I hear this same request coming up to me here now, and I cannot but be brief.

Although I stand for the younger generation here to-day, I am yet a lover of old times, old places, old faces and old memories. Everything that has power to win the abiding respect and obedience of men must have the springs of its being deep in the past, and it seems to me a most fortunate thing for us, the younger generation here represented, that our lives run back to just such old towns as this, with their accumulated wealth of sacred associations and clustering memories; and to-day as old Windham sits here like a Queen Mother, garlanded in all the leafy loveliness of June, and calls her sons and daughters about her to celebrate her natal day, I deem it a matter of especial pride to be numbered among her children.

It is a great thing for a township or a nation to be able to look back to a race of founders and a principle of institution in which it may see the realized ideal of nobility. Scholars have grown old and blind in striving to put their hands on the very spots where bold men have spoken and brave men have died; and commemorations such as this, when the old traditions are revived, old friendships cemented, and the noble lives of our heroic age held up in loving remembrance, are faithful teachers of the lessons of the past. They are the very poetry of history, and we shall spend no day in all the year which we shall devote to a higher or more satisfying purpose.

It has been to us a day of ennobling retrospect. We have wiped the dust from the urns of the fathers and followed their story step by step in the faithful narration of the historians. We have stood beside those early ploughmen as they sowed the seed with prayerful tears; we have traced their lines of glory through all the vicissitudes of their wondrous pilgrimage to the season of their noble harvest, and in the uplift and inspiration of their lives of sacrifice and devotion to principle, we have risen to the heights of the sublime faith of Tennyson until we

> "Doubt not through the ages
> One increasing purpose runs,
> And the thoughts of men are widened
> With the process of the suns!"

But such a day must not be given up to congratulation and happy retrospect alone. In our admiration of the Past we must not forget the ever-living Present, and that unhorizoned Future—just beyond.

Are the traditions ended? Is our story done? Have we heard it all? We are sometimes told so! Ever since Oliver Goldsmith wrote his "Deserted Village" it has seemed to be the fashion to read in the tender melancholy of those lines to Fair Auburn the epitaph of the old New England towns, and to-day in particular, the materialistic and hustling spirit of the age, devoid of sentiment or finer feeling, flaunts itself with brazen boldness and tells us we are stranded on the hilltops and left behind, while the great stream and tide of the world's progress rushes by!

This, it seems to me, is the narrowest, and shallowest, the most paltry and trifling and altogether unworthy utterance of these latter days. Why, Sir, it took two hundred years of training in the hard school of oppression in the old world—from Magna Charta down to Cromwell, and on to that fateful night when the Mayflower led her "star-guided furrow" out upon the waves of the "astonished sea"—to mould, and fashion, and temper the spirit of the men who founded these old townships! They established and vindicated here the principles of representative government and laid deep, and sure, and for all time, the foundations of a mighty state, with no king but an upright conscience, and upon whose bright banner was inscribed that new legend of promise that the seat of authority should be in the breasts of freemen!

The world knows their story all by heart. Their work was nobly conceived and grandly done, but we who inherit the fruits of their labors—our work is but just begun!

The fathers have fought the wars, cleared the forests, subdued the country and opened the way to this day of wonderful, surpassing prosperity. Ours are "the piping times of peace," a day of great industrial activity. An intensely materialistic spirit is rampant among us, the whole country seems to have spontaneously organized itself into a great modern pilgrimage of "Jason in search of the golden fleece." Our nation has followed the westward course of empire until it has laid hands on both oceans and levied tribute there, and we are to-day the granary, the workshop and the political hope of the world! Our accomplishments of material prosperity are stupendous and inspiring, but the inevitable responsibilities which go hand in hand with such endowments should give us pause. We should ask ourselves whether we are not tending to become a nation of men of one idea, bounding our horizon by the rim of the almighty dollar, whether we are not in danger of thinking altogether too much of tariff and silver and cotton and spindles, and too little of the bright ideals on which our national life is founded! There are feelings dearer than interest. There is a consummation more devoutly to be wished than mere material gain!

We are to-day sixty millions of people occupying a country capable of sustaining six hundred millions. By far the larger portion of our people have no common ancestry in the Revolution or the early days. Colonists are pouring in upon us from the states of the old world, bringing with them the languages and customs and intuitions of the Fatherland, and bringing with them their moss-grown prejudices and their political diseases too. Once here citizenship is easy—altogether too easy, it seems to me, Mr. President—and each raw immigrant speedily becomes part of the sovereign mind and will. In the new states of the far West only one-fifth to one fourth of the citizens are natives, and this great, swelling tide of new citizenship must be taught to organize its communities on the basis here first worked out, and to meet every question of national import in the true American spirit! In the solution of the pressing problems of our day, the sheet-anchor of the Ship of State is the trained intelligence and clear-eyed patriotism of those whose inheritance is here! The South through her tears and in the new-born hope of a better day looks to us to preserve the stately models of the past; the mighty West sings with her teeming harvests because she knows that here, on these old hills, the securities of conservatism go hand in hand with the hope of progress!

Such then is the high privilege, such the mission and the happy duty of the old New England township in these latter days—though sketched but dimly. We are the nearest of the children to the homes of the Fathers. To us it is given to guard their sacred graves, to bear their honored names and to hold up to the emulation of the nation their simple, steadfast lives!

The mission of these old towns can never be completely fulfilled while we have a country which needs to be taught their lessons of faith and constancy and devotion. To us is given as a sacred trust the legacy of those simple, sturdy days of "high thinking and plain living," to us the treasuring churchyard, the old schoolhouse, the old mill, to us all the sweet and tender influences of those far-off days, to us the sober melody of the "church going bell" and the "Cotter's Saturday night"! Is it not a priceless inheritance? Let us guard it well! For so, and so only, shall we in any measure repay the debt which the present generation owes to the Future. So shall conflicts of material interests be blended in happy compromise, and so, in the words of another, shall "the faith of the Fathers and the kindled imagination of the Sons unite us in a grand and noble ideal of the Great Republic."

"HEARSAY."

[RESPONSE BY CHARLES SMITH ABBE.]

In attempting to gather for oratorical purposes the minutes of a period embracing two centuries of this town's history, one is impressed with the amount of disconnected material furnished by historical documents. The preceding gentlemen have rendered a continuity of thought so admirably that for me to ask you over the ground again seems but to assume the role of plagiarist; but there are links in the chain which need strengthening, so I beg your attention for a little, fully aware of the delicate ground I am treading.

Just one word before our retrospect. I feel it my bounden duty to explain how I am here, *if I can*.

My first intimation of this bi-centennial was a card mailed me, to a suburb of Windham (Boston) about the 23rd of May, by your honorable president, asking if I would assist at the obsequies. I consented, as I had before painted and decorated towns, although not aware my reputation was so national.

Almost immediately upon arrival, I saw there had been an oversight—my name was not on the card. President Smith had received my letter of acceptance—I could not understand it. I must get into print somewhere. I made known my desire to your president; he would see what could be done. A few hours later I was waited on by several gentlemen of the honorary committee, and requested to furnish them proof I was a descendant of Old Windham, that being the open sesame to the card. They had been into the cemetery and copied every name there,—mine was not on the list. I insisted Abbe was among the number, but to no avail. I appealed to them as a body—No! I appealed to them as descendants—No!! I asked them to recognize me as one who had made some name for the town away from home; positively, No!!! I began to think the celebration would be a failure, when luckily I read Mr. William Wales's name. I drew him aside and said, "Mr. Wales, you have known me from the time of Moses; can you honestly say my name should not be on that list?"

"Charlie," said he, "I admit that you are one of us, but I've heard say one of your ancestors stole a sheep from the minister, took it the next morning to him and tried to pay his church tax with it, so of course I could not consent to have such occurrences brought to light by people discovering the name Abbe on the card, especially among the honorary committee."

I then tried the reception committee,—they knew the story; also the finance committee. I almost succeeded in getting in there, but at the last moment Mr. H. Hatch said he'd "rather give five dollars than have my name with his'n." So I moved on. The programme committee—Well, I had some choice—I didn't care to be with them. The collation committee I am sorry I ever saw. The relic committee—here is where I do get in, for surely I can prove I am a relic. I saw the lady and gentlemen relics, and said, "Allow me to enter your body, I am Mr. Charles Abbe. I—I—," "Yes, yes, that is all an old story, by what proof do you support your desire to become one of us?" I said, "Allow me to ask in return, how does, well, say Mr. Guilford Smith, support his claim?" They answered, "Why he is one of the best preserved relics we have, being loaned us by the Smithsonian Institute at Washington, D. C.," etc., etc., till finally I gave up trying to prove I was even a relic.

So I enter your midst under my own head, "Amusement Committee" entire, and call my subject "Hearsay," for this reason: I gleaned my information from a gentleman whose name you are all familiar with, but whose personal acquaintance extended to only the four hundred of Windham's oldest families. I refer to Mr. John Cates.

My great, great, grandfather—I omit two adjectives for all my Grandpa Abbes were great,—had a formal acquaintance with John Cates, but I think no one was chummy enough with Johnnie to swap stories as I did *en route* here this morning. It came about this way:

I started at 2 a. m., knowing how limited would be accommodations, but at the next similar celebration I shall start even earlier, as there must have been some who didn't go to bed at all; for upon arrival I found every seat taken, and [looking at watch] I've been standing all this time.

To resume, as I crossed the New London Northern tracks, I was accosted by a person of singular mien, pale and haggard, dressed in Puritanical costume, high conical wide-brimmed hat, long cloak, under which I discerned, collar and cuffs, brown jacket, knee breeches, broad shoes, with buckles, and who said, "Illustrious stranger, art travelling far?"

"Less than a league, and would be pleased to have company to yonder town." Before we crossed the Hartford track he had said, "Bless me, how things change," seven times, and then in a tone of perfect politeness he continued in words and manner of a by-gone age, but which for brevity and diction I will deliver modern.

"I am the original John Cates. I came here from Norwich. I slept in my cave till an hour ago, when my colored man, Joe Ginne, informed me it was time to be on the move if I wished to get a seat."

"My reason also,"—I interrupted.

"Indeed," said he, "I am bound for the Hither Place, I settled there in 1688."

Taking care to note that he had thoroughly finished, I said, "I am the original Charles Smith Abbe. I came here from Boston. I slept in a brass bedstead 'till an hour ago, when my electric clock told *me* I was to be on the move! I am bound for the Hither Place. You settled it in 1688; well, *I'm going to settle it to-day!*"

We rode as far as the brick house with Mr. John Staniford, when Mr. Cates suggested we were early enough to walk, and that he would enliven the time with stories. I consented also, and we alighted.

"Let us pause here until I recover my bearings," said he. "Ah, yes, there is Lot No. 1, owned by John Mason. In 1730 this lot passed into the possession of the Abbe family, and was the homestead of one of the most noted of the families of old Windham." [I quote from Mr. Weaver's history for the benefit of the honorary committee, who attempted to socially ostracise me.] "Lot No. 2 Hugh Calkins owned. Jonathan Crane bought that. Lot No. 3, I bought of Daniel Mason. When I took it the land was poor, but I labored early and late, and had the satisfaction of getting a good yield. One year in particular, I remember, I pulled up a single beet and bricked up the hole for a well. Another summer I had Joe out all night watching squashes—the vines grew so fast they would wear the squash all away dragging it over the ground."

"Pardon me," I interrupted—"but do you remember, Mr. Cates, whether in that translation of the Bible issued during the reign of that most gracious sovereign King James, any mention was made of the fate of Ananias?"

I think I have before remarked that Mr. Cates and I were chummy, but at this point Mr. Cates's stories seemed to be illustrating the saying, "Young men *think* the old ones are fools, but the old men *know* the young ones are."

"The Rev. Samuel Whiting, Windham's first minister," Mr. Cates continued, "whose residence was near the Green, once told me of a most amusing mistake he made on the second day of his arrival in the Colony. The two Mason families had met with a loss at the same time, but of much difference in character. One had lost an old family horse, the other the husband and father. Mr. Whiting knew of the decease of the husband, but not of the horse.

"As he informed me, newly settled here, and over anxious to perform his consoling duty, he called on the family who had lost the horse, supposing all the while he was with the bereaved ones. The lady of the house received the new minister with great cordiality, highly pleased with the honor of the first call; and encouraged by his welcome, our reverend, after the usual formal salutations, said:

" 'Sister, my condolence is yours, you have certainly met with a great loss, but I trust you will not be utterly cast down.'

" 'Yes, indeed, I have; he was so faithful and trustworthy, and if I do say it, there wasn't a better one in the place.'

" 'So I've heard, and so regular in his attendance at church.'

" 'Yes, I drove him to church nearly every Sunday.'

" 'Drove him! I beg your pardon, I supposed he would attend of his own accord, without being driven.'

" 'Well, of late years I never took the whip to him, for he was not so lively as he used to be, in fact, no one could ever call him fast.'

"Our minister could not laugh at this grim joke. He started to say, 'Madam, I—' but she broke in with, 'It wasn't often, but sometimes, old as he was, he got frisky, and then I'd have to curb him.'

" 'I have heard him spoken of as the patient martyr.'

" 'Patient? Yes, but there were times when the colt would crop out in him, and then I'd have to cut down his feed, and he would soon come to time.'

" 'What a Xantippe I am dealing with,' thought our reverend, but he only said, 'Madam, it is the way of all that has life.' But our sister broke in with,—'But withal he was so gentle and kind, his good qualities outweighed his faults; I felt I must keep him for the good he had done.'

" 'Keep him! Good he had done!'

" 'Some of my friends advised me to get rid of him, for he was considerable trouble and expense.'

"Mr. Whiting was so nonplussed, he could only stutter, 'Death must have been a welcome release.'

" 'Oh, yes, of course, and it might have been a mercy if he had died younger.'

" 'What!'

"But the sister capped the climax when she said, 'Now that he is gone I miss him; anything that has come into our lives, a care, we miss, but I can find another, and possibly one that will be of more service to me.'

" 'More service to you! Madam, your depravity appalls me! How you can sit there and speak so of one hardly cold in his grave is past my comprehension. It seems you need no consolation for the death of your husband.'

" 'Husband! Who said anything about my husband? I've been talking about old Dobbin, a horse we've had since we came to Windham.'

"Mutual explanations followed, and the madam and the Reverend Mr. Whiting were fast friends for life."

"Mr. Cates, is there any truth to what you've been telling?"

"Well," and his eyes glistened with laughter, "I've heard say."

"Mr. Cates," I said, "for a man of your years this walk and the stories must be using you up. They are me. And now that we have reached the Green, let me speak of the Windham of modern times. The street intersecting the one we came on, or as you know it 'Nipmuck Path', is the old stage coach thoroughfare from Boston to Hartford. I said modern times, yes, for aside from the unlimited power of electricity we have progressed from the Indian's trail to the stage coach propelled by the horse, to the locomotive by steam, 'till now, with this new power in its infancy, when by a single strand of wire, we are able to travel a mile a minute; and if we both attend the next bi-cententennial, we shall probably be able to come here by the air line.

"So in smaller, or shall I say, larger scope, we see the advance of the town.

"Fifty years ago there were fourteen stores facing this

Green; to-day all swallowed up in that modern idea, the Syndicate, controlled in this instance by Mr. Chester Woodworth!

"The churches, in 1820 Windham had three, but their work was so efficacious, their revivals so complete, their action so harmonious, that to-day we have only one open regularly, and it is expected by another Christmas, even that will be closed, and we can then rely wholly upon the Sunday papers.

"And now Mr. Cates,"—Ladies and Gentlemen, as I seem to have lost Mr. Cates,—we are congregated here upon the Hub of Windham on this occasion. Our closing thought is of this Hub, this old Green, this Windham Green. If it could speak it could tell more stories than Mr. John Cates. It might say, "I have seen the time of the Indian, the Puritan, the reverend father, the bull-frog fright, the excitement over the stamp act, Bunker Hill, marching of the men to Boston, Parson White and his daughter's gift, celebration of the independence of the colonies, Washington's death, events of the War of 1812, War with Mexico, barbecues, Thanksgiving shooting matches, where the participants left the field in a condition best expressed by that line of Longfellow's, "Oh little feet I'm weary, thinking of your load"; the Bank robbery, the call to arms in '61, Emancipation proclamation, Lincoln's assassination, peace again, and now this, the latest public occasion.

I spoke in the beginning of the links which needed strengthening. I am one of those links, we are all links in that chain, which at the end has the anchor, Windham. We need such occasions as this to strengthen our love, and bind our hearts together, and after we have had communion together, what more fitting than that Windham, Old Windham in her gray hairs, should have the last word;

"Listen! children all, sons and daughters of those gone before;

I say to you as I said to them:

"In youth I fostered you, in manhood I applauded you;
In age I say to you, grow old along with me;
The best is yet to be,
The last of life for which the first was made:
Our times are in His hands who saith, 'The whole I planned.'
Youth shows but half; trust God; see all, nor be afraid.'"

WILLIMANTIC IN EIGHTEEN FIFTY.

[Compiled by Allen B. Lincoln for the Bi-Centennial but not read for lack of time, and now published by request of the Committee.]

I wish to give you a picture of Willimantic as it was about the year 1850, at the height of its growth and prosperity as a "Factory village," at the beginnings of the days of the railroad, and showing the foundations on which the present growth to extensive manufacturing, and the beginnings of an educational center, has been reared. Follow me with your mind on the Willimantic of to-day, and you will get a comparative picture of great interest. I do not lay claim to accuracy, but the picture is approximately correct, as to the chief features and families of the town at that date. I am indebted chiefly to General Lloyd E. Baldwin for information.

At the west end, stood the Windham Company's mills and store substantially as they are now, with the "Savings Institute" in the second story of the store building; and the six houses of the "Yellow row" beyond, and the "White row" on Main street opposite. Just west of the store on Main street stood Agent A. C. Tingley's residence, a pretentious mansion in those days, now the home of Agent Thomas C. Chandler. North-east of "White Row," and near the present site, stood the First district school house. Away at the west end, as now, stood alone in the wilderness the Hardin Fitch place, occupied then as now by him, and one of the oldest houses, if not the oldest, in town. Between the "White row" and the Hardin Fitch place there were scattered a dozen or fifteen houses, among which were the residences of Deacon D.

Terry, occupied now as then by him; opposite him lived William H. Cranston, in the house now occupied by his grandson, Allen L. Cranston ; next east on the corner of Hooper's Lane (now Winter street) lived Harry Boss; a few rods east lived Warren Atwood, and nearly opposite from him, in the house now the second east of Mansfield avenue, lived Dr. Asahel Tarbox.

Over the river, at the west end of what is now Pleasant street, was the principal residence district. Then as now the first house east of "Card Road," stood the spacious white mansion of Stephen Hosmer, afterwards the home of William H. Hosmer, his son, and of James Martin, "the old sexton." At what is now the northwest corner of Bridge and Pleasant streets, stood the toll gate, which even in 1850 had fallen into "innocuous desuetude," but whose old red toll-house has been torn down within only a few years past, and its ruined foundations are still to be seen. About opposite the toll-house lived Thomas Jordan, brother of Lyman, in the house now modernized and occupied by George Tiffany. Elisha Burnham lived where his son Abel now lives, and Ralph Williams lived in the house now occupied by Samuel G. Adams. Further down Pleasant street was the James D. Hosmer residence, still occupied by his daughter; then the home of Fred Campbell, now occupied by Conductor Edward Stone; then the home of General L. E. Baldwin, now occupied by E. F. Reed. Next came William Morrison's little brick house, also still standing, and occupied to-day by James N. Bailey.

Down on the main road towards the bridge (Bridge street) came the house built by George W. Manahan, occupied later by the Rev. Samuel G. Willard, and then by Chauncey Turner, the present occupant ; then the old "Eagle house," built by William Porter in 1833, and afterwards occupied successively by Jefferson Campbell, and his brother, Thomas Campbell, the latter dying there ; and next north Miss Sarah Porter's place, now occupied by William C. Cargell. The street has been much cut down, as plainly appears. On what is now River street stood first on the south side the Stephen Bromley place, and all the houses on that side now occupied by the King family, Alonzo Green, Judge Wheeler and George B. McCracken, and on the other side of the street, as now, lived Ira Sweetland, and also the late Deacon Luther Martin of the M. E. Church.

From the junction of River and Pleasant streets east there was then no house until we reach that now occupied by Lawyer John L. Hunter, then next east was Deacon A. H. Fuller's home, now occupied by his widow and after her bequeathed to become the Baptist parsonage; Edwin H. Hall lived next east in the house lately sold to E. S. Page by George Lincoln; opposite stood then as now the Alfred Youngs place; then no house to the east until we reach what is now the "boarding house" on the high knoll, and which in 1850 was the spacious residence of Asa Jillson. Next east was the Joseph C. Bassett place, then as now occupied by him; next east the home of Josiah Dean, Jr.; then the old Hebard tavern, now a tenement house; nearly opposite was the residence of Col. William Jillson, now occupied by his son, William C. Jillson; then diagonally southeast across the street, as now, the Tingley house, and next east the house of Lawyer Joel R. Arnold, now occupied by Charles R. Utley. Next on the north side came the house of Col. Roswell Moulton, where now his son John H. Moulton lives. Next east of him dwelt Ulysses Young then, and now his widow.

Nearly opposite, and next east of Judge John M. Hall's present residence, and where now Superintendent John Scott of the Linen Company lives, dwelt in 1850 Seth Jillson, and later Allen B. Burleson. Then the turnpike stretched away towards Old Windham, with the Anson Young place, then a small red house (now supplanted by a large double frame dwelling), and the Josiah Dean (now Earl Cranston's) place, and the Deacon Eleazer Bill place, in recent years known as the "Maple House," between Willimantic's outskirts and Natchaug river on the Windham road;—so it appears that this region has not changed much since 1850.

Now let us return to the west end, and start with the Smithville Company's mills, which were flourishing in 1850, with their stone row alongside the railway track, and the white row on south side of Main street and the two houses built by Deacon Lee. On the corner of Main and what is now Bridge street stood their supply store, in the basement of the building, to-day unoccupied, but the main portion of the building was then as now, a boarding or tenement house. West of what is now Carpenter Bros., in "School House Lane," dwelt Israel Robinson, next east "Aunt Lucy Crane," and about on the present site of Carpenters' store was the house of Robert Prentice; then came the house of Azariah Lathrop, with Laban Chase's shoe store in the basement.

On the northwest corner of Main and High Streets dwelt Laban Chase, in the house now there standing. On the opposite corner of High street was the Elias Rathburn place, later known as the home of Dr. William Witter, the first long-resident physician of Willimantic. High street was open at this time. Robert Hooper's house was the first one built on that street and was then as now occupied by him. Next south of him Wightman Williams lived, in the house now owned and occupied by Edmund Crane. Egbert Hall and later Samuel B. Ford and Courtland Babcock lived successively in the house lately bought and remodelled by Robert Truscott. James Sterry lived in in the little house opposite Robert Hooper's, and George P. Heap, afterwards husband of Mrs. Kellogg of Heap will fame, built and occupied the house lately vacated by Giles H. Alford, northeast corner of Valley and High streets.

Returning now on Main street, next below the Rathburn or Witter place on the site of the present Levi Frink block, but in the cottage now standing rear of Frink's block, dwelt Nathan Fish, father of Angeline Fish, who lately died at the age of eighty years or more. Next dwelt William

F. Essex, in the house which stood on the site where Farley's new building is now going up. Next was the Nathan Hall place, a brick block now occupied for stores beneath and tenements above, and which in 1850 was occupied for a short time by Parson Willard and wife of the Congregational church. Then came the Thomas Cunningham residence, that large white building occupied in recent years by Archambeault's store beneath and tenements above; and next east of this, near what is now the Walnut street corner, stood in 1850 Thomas Cunningham's grog shop. There was then no Walnut street, and all north of Main street in this section was meadow and forest.

Then a few rods east again stood the first Dr. Witter place, built for him in 1831, but in 1850 and until his death in 1885 the home of Horace Hall, for many years a leading citizen and father of his honor, Judge John M. Hall of to-day. The house is now occupied by John M. Gray, the bill poster. Next stood the little Harrington house on the site of Thomas Haran's new block. Then Niles Potter's hotel, called then the Tremont house, now Young's hotel.

Let us cross now to the south side, and just opposite Potter's hotel was Stephen Kimbel's house, (now replaced by the new Kimbel block) and in the little one-story addition to his house Stephen Kimbel sat for many years as the village shoe-maker. The old building next east now occupied as a saloon was then a store, and occupied at times by different parties, of whom John G. Keigwin was one, he having begun the clothing business there.

Next east was the old Congregational Church, now remodelled into Meloney's block; then came George C. Elliott's house and tailor shop and the famous little twin-buildings, on the sites now occupied by the Arnold and Chapman blocks respectively. Then the old Franklin building, a large frame structure, the first public building in Willimantic, built by Gen. Baldwin in 1847 and in 1850 occupied by William L. Weaver's book-store, L. & H. Feldman's dry goods house (afterwards Alpaugh and

Hooper's); and Lawyers Joel R. Arnold and Jairus H. Carpenter had offices in the second story, while in the third was a hall for public gatherings. East of the Franklin building there was in 1850 nothing south of Main street but an alder swamp (save the old brick depot of dingy memory which stood about fifty feet south of the present station) until you came to the "old stone row" of tenement houses belonging to the Jillson mill, and which then stood near the river shore a few rods southwest of the present Main street railway crossing. There was no broad Railroad street then — only a lane to the depot in the swamp!

Returning to the Potter hotel (now Young's hotel), the building next east, on the north side of the street, was a little shop on the site of the present Hooker house, built by Albert Sherman, "gentleman fashioner," as his sign read, and afterwards occupied by General Baldwin with the post office. Bank street was not thought of and all back of it was swamp near by, and forest in the distance. Jairus Littlefield's house stood where the Savings Institute now is; then Mrs. Lavinia Loomis's house, where the United Bank Building now is; then the house occupied now as then by Melancthon Turner, and the late Isaac Wilson, with the livery stable in the rear as now. The old William C. Boon place, (now Dr. Card's Block) came next, and then, on the site of the present opera house, stood the junior Chester Tilden's little candy and fruit shop, right on the corner of Main street and Tanner's lane, (now North street); and high up on the bank, behind the little shop, stood the senior (Rev.) Chester Tilden's dwelling house. Tanner's lane led up a sharp hill and then down again to the old slaughter house, which then stood where Johnson's livery stable now is, and a part of which was afterwards worked into the building of Warren Tanner's (now Johnson's) livery. Across the lane from Chester Tilden's stood the dwelling house built by Samuel Barrows in 1828 and in 1850 owned by General Baldwin, afterwards bought by Warren Tanner and gradually enlarged to the present

Tanner Block. Then came Dr. Jason Safford's drug store in a little building afterwards enlarged by L. J. Fuller and Son to its present size, and where Frank Wilson and Company's Pharmacy, in direct line of succession, still dispenses drugs as did Dr. Safford of old, and his predecessors Messrs. Alfred Howes, John A. Perkins and Newton Fitch, the last named of whom founded the store in 1828.

Next stood the original M. E. church, which about this time was removed to Church street and became the old Christian boarding house, lately supplanted by Johnsons' new block now occupied by Perkins and Blish; and the old church site on Main street was soon occupied by the Atwood Block built by Warren Atwood; and in 1850 the new M. E. Church was built, on the present site on Church street, thus giving the street its name.

Next east of the old church on Main street, stood the building now known as the Brainard house, the main part of which was built by Sheffield Lewis in 1848, and was in 1850 occupied by stores and for tenements, but was soon afterwards bought by Henry Brainard and by him made into a hotel bearing the present name. Next east of the Lewis (now Brainard) building, the corner lot (present site of the "Windham" hotel) was then vacant, and on the site of the present Commercial Block stood the mansion of Joshua B. Lord;—the house has since been removed and is now standing on Turner street opposite James Walden's residence.

I well remember that old Lord mansion. It stood well back from the street, with portico and bay windows, marvellous luxuries for those days, and in front was a lawn varied by shrubbery and flower beds, while along the street line was a handsome hedge, the whole making a picture to my childish eyes which only the word "grandeur" could adequately convey. Here dwelt Marian Lord, the sole heiress of her father's (Daniel Lord's) score or more of thousands, and she died on what was to have been her wedding day, at the age of eighteen, and they buried her with her diamond ring on. Her father had died some time before, and her broken-hearted grandmother, Eunice Richmond Kellogg, her nearest of kin, sought legal advice to retain as a keepsake a fine old lace shawl which she and Marian had worn together, but which other claimants to the estate had taken, with all the rest of the property. Mrs. Kellogg found that she was the rightful heir, not only to the shawl keepsake, but to all of Marian's property, and she thus came into possession of it. In after years she married George P. Heap, the English tailor; and after his death E. McCall Cushman became her advisor, counsellor and friend, and she finally left to him the property, which by the accidents of death had been diverted from the Lord line that accumulated it, to entirely foreign channels. Hence arose the famous Heap will case, or Richmond's appeal from probate, so lately "settled out of court," after two fruitless trials.

Next east of the Lord mansion stood the Baptist church, on its present site. Then came the Hanover block, still standing, and where in 1850 George W. Hanover and Thomas Turner carried on the millinery and dry goods business, and manufactured hoop-skirts. Later Mrs. Hanover conducted the business, calling her place the "Temple of Fashion;" hence the name of Temple street. Then came the James Howes place, now remodeled into the double-verandahed dwelling house on the corner of Union and Center streets.

At the junction of Main and Union streets, where now stands the Cushman block, there stood about 1850 a small shop.

About opposite the Hanover building on Union street stood Dr. William K. Otis's little office building, where patients sought him for many years; and the same building may be found standing to-day on the southwest corner of Temple and Valley streets. Next beyond Dr. Otis's office was a stretch of grass land to the old Fitch house, to-day standing as the big and dingy white tenement house opposite A. B. Adams's; then came the Cushman residence, now owned as a tenement by Durkee, Stiles &

Co., but then the home of J. E. Cushman, who has now removed to California.

A few rods to the east of Mr. Cushman's stood the stone mansion of William Jillson, standing to-day just north of the Main street railroad crossing, and then called one of the finest residences in town. Next east of the Howes place on Union street was a stretch of meadow to the house now occupied by Mrs. Vilatia Loomer and Dr. C.|H. Colgrove, but about 1850 occupied by Capt. Roger Gurley and Joseph Woodward. Then came the house now occupied by Charles Bliven; next the house occupied for many years by Merrick Johnson, and still standing, but now set back from the road. On the corner of Union and Jackson streets was the store of Roderick Davison, later the firm of Davison and (John H.) Moulton.

In all the region north of Main street, and between High and Jackson streets, there stood in 1850, besides the old slaughter house and the M. E. church already mentioned, only two houses;—one that of Davis Weaver, grandfather of Editor Thomas Snell Weaver, (it was here that our "Journal" editor was born) and at this time the house was occupied by Zelotes Chaffee, and to-day is the home of Frank S. Fowler at the corner of Maple avenue and Bellevue street ; the other was the George Bull place, so-called, the little white cottage still standing next east of James McAvoy's residence. All the rest of this great tract, now so thickly settled, was a swampy valley with a brook running through it, (the brook still runs but now into our sewers) and stretched away up the hillside into chestnut forests and wild fields. "Prospect street" was not dreamed of and "Summit street" and "Lewiston avenue" and the rest, were unimaginable !

On Jackson street, the first house, now standing, on the east side, was the Jesse Wilson place. Abel Clark lived in the first house on the west side, now owned by William F. Gates. The house now so long owned by William H. Osborn was built and then occupied by Sidney Brewster. The house now standing next north of Montgomery hose house was the home of John Chipman, for many years night watchman for the Jillsons. Across the street east from what is now Grant's grain store stood the Douglas Vaughn place, the same house still remaining. The site of Grant's store was then a lawn studded with shade trees and behind it stood the house of William Branch, who afterwards went to Utah and became a Mormon priest. This house became the home of Editor William L. Weaver of "The Journal," and on the hill to the west of it stood for many years a magnificent tall and widespreading oak, the solace of his later years, but which the advent of Loomer's lumber yard in 1865 destroyed, to the great personal grief of Mr. Weaver.

On the site of the present Catholic church stood the house of Capt. Calvin Davison, brother of Roderick, and nearly opposite was the home of the venerable Luke Flynn, father of Willimantic's present superintendent of streets, of the same name ; and the old Flynn house stands to-day just off the Mansfield road near the little bridge beyond Whittemore park watering-trough. Henry Youngs lived where John Hickey now lives and William Godfrey lived in James Murray's present house. Albert Moulton lived where he does now, and Jackson, the colored man from whom the street was named, and who was a respected citizen here for many years, lived in the white cottage which stood until lately on the site of John Killourey's present house, but is now moved to the rear of the latter. Mr. Jackson at that time held the whole of the Hewitt property (to-day so-called), and which has lately been opened and been developed into a residence district, and it was of Mr. Jackson that Mr. Hewitt secured this land.

There were no other houses north of the Hewitt and Jackson property until you came to the old stone house now at the cross roads of Ash and Jackson streets, and which was then the Nathaniel Robinson place, and later the Gordon place. To the west on the north side of Chestnut-hill road stood the Calvin Robinson place, then a red house, but since painted white, and to-day known as the Whittemore place, and on the south side, the Luther Robinson place, still to be seen as "the old red house." No other houses were in this region in 1850.

Passing now down the south-east road (Ash street) from Jackson street, we come first to the old Carey place occupied in 1850 by John Smith and now by his son James. Next on the east side lived Joseph Rollinson in the house now made over into the "Hawthorne" on the same site. Next on the north side up Main street, on the northeast corner of Main and what is now Brook street still stands the house where Scott Smith, brother of John, lived in 1850. Across the road and on the south side and around the corner towards the mill is to-day the same row of white tenement houses that Jillson and Capen owned in 1850, and farther to the south by the river was their mill, now the Linen Co.'s No. 3. The old Capen homestead, first built and occupied by Loren Carpenter, first warden of the borough, stood where it does now, just east of Hennesey's store, and was until he died in 1890, the home of John H. Capen. The present site of the Linen Company's "New Village" was then a stretch of hillside and valley and swamp.

Now come back to Union street, where we left it at Jackson. First on the north side below Jackson stood, as now, the two-tenement house, then owned by Lucian Clark, and next east was the residence of Maxon G. Clark, now occupied by his widow and her daughter, Mrs. J. C. Robinson. Next came the Ahab Wilkinson place, occupied in 1850 by Mr. Wilkinson's aunts and the widow of Dr. Kingsley, and now by the Chamberlain family. Then came the house of Elisha Williams' the large house now standing at the corner of Union and Milk streets; and east across Milk street was the home of Ephraim Herrick, the pioneer truckman, which is still standing.

Directly across Union street south from the Herrick house still stands the house where lived in 1850 Addison Safford, whose blacksmith shop was down across the lot to the southeast near the "old stone school house." Now draw an air line from Addison Safford's house to Col. William Jillson's (now William C. Jillson's) residence, and follow beneath it until you go about half way to the river, and you will stand about where, on a rocky knoll, was the site of the famous "old stone school house," which in 1850 was at the height of its fame. The road did not run where it does now, but after coming north across the river, forked at the river side, leading east along the bank to Jillson & Capen's mill, and north-west gradually away from the river up by William Jillson's stone house, about as now.

To the east of the school house along the site of the present No. 2 mill was the combination paper, grist and saw mill successively owned by Clark & Gray, Smith & Byrne and Col. George Spafford, but in 1850 owned by a Mr. Campbell of New York and run by Page & Son. To the inland about opposite the present office of the Linen Company stood two or three dwelling houses. What is now the Linen Company's spool shop at the foot of Jackson street was then the chief mill of A. & S. Jillson. Just to the east by the river bank stood the old Duck mill and next east of that but west of the site of the present No. 1 mill, stood another three-story mill of the Jillsons, but both it and the Duck mill have been removed. No. 1 was not built until 1857 and then by the Linen Company. Opposite the Jillson mill,—now the spool shop—was the old stone store where the employees traded. Next east was the store and dwelling of George Byrne.

Then came the old Universalist church elsewhere referred to ; then next east the building now at the northwest corner of Main and Washington streets, occupied above as a dwelling and in the basement by the general store of Waterman C. and Lucian H. Clark. On the opposite corner of Washington street corner was Edward Moulton's drug store. George Lathrop (now of Windham Centre) kept a general store in the building now occupied by Edward F. Casey's furniture house. The houses still standing along to the east were occupied as dwellings, that next to Lathrop's then by Joanna Wilkinson, an elderly maiden lady, now by George Wheeler, the prompter ; the next by Martin Harris then, now a tenement house.

This section along Main street in front of the Jillson mills and along by the foot of Washington street, was known as "Exchange Place." On the south side of Exchange Place, towards the river, stood the old "hay scales." The post-office had been removed by Gen. L. E. Baldwin from Col. Roswell Moulton's store, which then stood at the fork of the roads near the river, uptown to the little store opposite Potter's hotel (now Young's,) and the tendency of commercial growth was that way.

Such, practically, was the Willimantic of 1850.

THE EXHIBITION OF RELICS.

[On the day of the Bi-Centennial Celebration, a display of Relics was made in the old Windham Bank building. Following is a list of the articles exhibited, with the names of the persons who loaned them set opposite.]

ARTICLES.	LOANED BY
Carved Oak Chest, (date 1696)	Mrs. Warren Elliott.
Wooden Canteen,	" " "
Iron Candlesticks,	Jairus Smith.
Silhouettes of Mr. and Mrs. Jairus Smith, Sr.,	" "
Alfred Avery Burnham, (portrait)	Mrs. Ardelia Burnham Smith.
Washington's Courtship, "	Mrs. Andrew Frink.
Mr. Moses Abbe "	" " "
Mrs. Talitha Waldo Abbe, "	" "
Coverlet,	Mrs. Charles E. Spencer.
Coverlet,	Mrs. Charles Larrabee, Jr.
Indian Relics,	Thomas C. Waterous
Watch—Owned by the Rev. Charles Larrabee, a Huguenot pastor, who escaped with a portion of his flock from the south of France, during the massacre which followed the revocation of the Edict of Nantes, Oct. 16, 1685, and landed at Baltimore, Md. Thus it has been in this country over two hundred years.	Charles Larrabee, Sr.
Coat of Arms, (Larrabee)	" "
Miss Julia Ripley, (portrait) Artist, Mr. George Cushman,	Charles Larrabee, Sr.
Painting,	Miss Ida Spafford.
Sampler,(by Mrs. Martha Perkins Johnson,(date 1773),	" "
Hand Fire Screen,	" "
Capt. George A. Fisher's Sword.	" "
Silver Spoons, (date 1790)	" "
Coverlet,	" "
Old Newspapers, one published in Norwich at the time of Washington's death, and containing an account of the funeral services,	" "

| ARTICLES. | LOANED BY. |

Suit of Clothes, sword and sash, worn by Captain Adam Larrabee (then lieutenant) while he was engaged in the attack at La Colle, Canada, under General Wilkinson, March 30, 1814. During this engagement, he was shot through the lungs, the bullet hole being visible in the coat and vest,   Henry Larrabee.
One Volume Josephus,   "   "
One Volume Lectures on the Scriptures, (two hundred years old),   "   "
United States Census, (date 1820)   "   "
Circular Arm Chair,   "   "
Silver Spoons,   Mrs. Julia Frink Arnold.
Silver Knee Buckles, (one hundred years old),   "   "
Toasting Iron,   "   "
Two brown Satin dresses, (one hundred years old),   Mrs. Henry Page.
Two Tortoise Shell Combs,   "   "
Two Calashes, (seventy five years old),   "   "
Half dozen sermons, preached by Parson White in 1760,   "   "
Cards of Invitation to balls at the old Staniford Tavern,
Spinning Wheel.   "   "
Silk Embroidery, (framed by Miss Maria Stoddard),   "   "
Chair, with circular arms, (seventy-five years old,   "   "
Zaccheus Waldo and wife, Esther Stevens Waldo, (portrait), taken on one canvas,   Mrs. Henry S. Walcott.
Mrs. Mary Abbe Taintor, (portrait),   "   "   "
Samuel Huntington Perkins,   "   Miss Charlotte Elderkin Clark.
Nancy Perkins Converse,   "   "   "   "
Tortoise Shell Comb,   "   "   "
John Staniford, (Portrait)   George Challenger.
Duke of Marlboro.   "   "   "
The Nativity,   "   "   "
George Washington,   "   Mrs. Mary Lathrop Ramsdell.
John Lathrop,   "   "   "
Coat-of-arms, (Lathrop)   "   "
Bacchus, God of Wine, (Painting) Artist, George B. Baldwin,   Guilford Smith.
Chauncey F. Cleaveland,   "   Mrs. Helen Cleaveland.
Chester Hunt, M. D.   "   Mrs. Delia Hunt Hebard.
George Washington,   "   Mrs. Fanny Hawkins.
The Seasons,   "   "   "
Martha Washington, (copy of an oil painting at the Capitol)   Mrs. Delia Hunt Hebard.
View of Windham in 1815,   Dr. Frank E. Guild.

ARTICLES.		LOANED BY.
View of Windham, (Oil)	1830	Dr. Henry Gray.
Zaccheus Waldo, (Portrait)		Mrs. Sarah Bingham Lathrop.
Nancy Waldo Bingham,	"	"
Goddess of Liberty	"	"

(Artist of these three, Samuel L. Waldo, a pupil of Benjamin West, London.)

Samuel Gray. (Portrait)		Dr. Henry Gray.
Charlotte Elderkin Gray,	"	" "
Rev. Ebenezer Devotion,	(Photo)	Mrs Francis Devotion Lathrop.
Martha Lathrop Devotion,	"	" "
Jonathan Devotion,	(Portrait)	" "
Duke of Marlboro,	"	" "
Duke of Cumberland,	"	" "
Coat-of-arms, Devotion)	"	" "
Judge Ebenezer Devotion,	(Portrait)	Gerald Waldo.
Mrs. Ebenezer Devotion and child,	"	" "
Devotion Brothers - three—John Jonathan, Ebenezer, "		"

Deed, Jonah Palmer.
Deed, (1737)
Record of Deaths, (1751-1814)
Green's Register, (1796)
Copies of Windham "Herald" (1st issue) March 12, 1791 to 1814,
New Testament, Mrs. Francis Devotion Lathrop. printed in London, in the reign of Elizabeth, in 1589 — with two translations - the Rhemes and the Church of England.
Letter—from the church in Wenham to the church in Windham; in behalf of John Abbee and Hannah Abbee, (his wife) and of Robert Hibbard and Mary Hibbard, (his wife) recommending them to the watch and care of the church in Windham. Joseph Gerrish, Pastor. Dated Wenham, Oct. 29, 1700.
Abstract. Capt. William Young's Company for the defence of New London in 1781.
Charter granted by His Majesty King Charles the Second.
Version of the Bible with illustrations (pen and ink) by Ebenezer Gray.
Sermon; Joseph Lothrop. 1811.
Sermon, Cornelius Everest, 1816.
Digest of the Laws of the State of Connecticut. (2 Vols.) • by Zephaniah Swift, L. L. D. C. A. S. 1823.
Diploma, to Samuel Gray from Dartmouth College.
Diploma to Samuel Huntington Devotion from Yale College.

ARTICLES.　　　　　　　　　　　LOANED BY.

Commission of Samuel Gray as Commissary General,
   signed by John Hancock.
Commission of Abner Lathrop, signed by George Washington.
Sermons, by Rev. Samuel Whiting January 1, 1693, and 1721.
Sermons, by Rev. Stephen White, April 14, 1760, April 3, 1764.
Petition of Windham and Chaplin, against removing the
   Courts from Windham,
The Epistle of the Apostle St. James, Resolved, Ex-
   pounded, and Preached upon by way of Doctrine and
   Use. For the benefit and instruction of all Christian
   people, and for the help and direction of young
   practisers in Theology; By John Mayer, Doctor of
   Divinity. Printed at London 1629.
   　　　　　　　　　　　Mrs. Francis Devotion Lathrop.
Warwick Castle.　　　　　　　Mrs. Harriett Gray Swift.
Edinboro' Castle,　　　　　　　　"　　　　"
Bed Curtain of white linen, spun, wove and embroidered
   in colors by Miriam Webb Ripley, in 1736,
   　　　　　　　　　　　Eunice S. Ripley.
Silver Tankard, (1747)　　　　　　"　　　　"
Wedding Dress of white linen, spun, wove and embroid-
   ered in colors by Mary Meyers in 1732,　　John Babcock.
Gun,　　　　　　　　　　　　George Lathrop.
Horse Pistol,　　　　　　　　　　"　　　　"
War Club, (Fejee)　　　　　　　　"　　　　"
An Old Musket, carried by one Durkee in the French
   and Indian war, from 1754 to 1759; afterwards was
   carried through the war of the Revolution by Tim-
   othy Kingsley; also carried by his son, Oramel
   Kingsley at New London in the war of 1812.
   　　　　　　　　　Captain William Moulton,
   　　　　　　　(Grandson of Timothy Kingsley.)
Sword, (Revolution)　　　　　Mrs. Mary Wyllys.
Sampler, (1742)　　　　　　　　"　　　　"
Reel and Flax,　　　　　　　　　"　　　　"
Blue China from Staniford Tavern,　　"　　　　"
Chair of Rev. Samuel Whiting, (1700)
   　　　　　　　Congregational Church of Windham.
Chair of Zaccheus Waldo,　　Mrs. Sarah Bingham Lathrop.
Chair of Mrs. Sibyl Backus Lathrop,　Mrs. Julia A. Swift.
Watch and Shoe Buckles of Judge Ebenezer Devotion,
   　　　　　　　　　Mrs. Francis Devotion Lathrop.
Looking Glass of Col. Eliphalet Dyer,　Mrs. Delia Hunt Hebard.
Pewter Platters, Porringer and Flagon,　Henry E. Staniford.

ARTICLES.	LOANED BY
Powder Horn,	Henry E. Staniford
Punch Bowl and China from Staniford's Tavern	" "
Fancy China Fruit Dishes on Stands, (1767)	Mrs. Elisha Avery.
Punch Bowl,	" "
Sugar Bowl,	" "
A Small Case of Drawers and Writing Desk, (1772)	" "
An Iron Fife, imported from Germany and used at the battle of Bunker Hill.	Mrs. Elisha Avery, (daughter of Solomon Loring.)
A Tea Pot, in which Tea was made on the sly, at the time of the Embargo,	Mrs. A. D. Loring
A Child's Rocking Chair of solid oak boards (107 years old) made by Zaccheus Waldo for his daughter Nancy Waldo,	Mrs. Sarah Bingham Lathrop.
Water color,	Mrs. Charlotte Gray Lathrop.
Water color,	Mrs. Hannah Gray Parsons.
The Widow,	Mrs. Gertrude Storrs Bissell.
Writing Desk, (1620)	Mr. Frink Hebard
China breakfast and tea set of Mary Gray (1812)	Mrs. Hariett Gray Swift.
China plate, subject "Landing of Lafayette in New York" (August 1824.)	Mrs. Charles E. Spencer.
China plate, Subject—"The University of Transylvania."	
Carved Image of Bacchus,	A. E. Brooks.
Call Bell from the Staniford Tavern,	" "
First Steam Railroad passenger Train in America on the Mohawk and Hudson R. R. (1831) Copy of an Oil Painting in the possession of the Connecticut Historical Society, Hartford, (2 copies)	Mr. William Palmer and Mr. Jairus Smith.
Silk embroidery, by Mary Gray,	Mrs. Harriett Gray Swift.
Silk embroidery, by Sally Allen,	Arthur S. Winchester.
China Plate, Subject, "The University of Transylvania,"	Mrs. Frances Devotion Lathrop.

CORRECTIONS AND ADDITIONS.

[The long delay in securing the photographs from which the illustrations of this volume are made, has afforded opportunity to note some slight errors in the printed text, and to add a few facts of interest, as herewith given.]

Page 4, Among the honorary vice-presidents, the names of Storrs Swift and Palmer Fenton belong to Mansfield, instead of Hampton.

Page 11, line 17, read Capt. Morrison, instead of Robinson.

Page 14, line 7, read June 10, instead of May 10.

Page 15, line 15, read Dr. Guild, instead of Dr. Smith.

Page 16. It should be understood that the poem of Miss Robbins was contributed to represent at the Bi-Centennial gathering the town of Chaplin, which sprang from Windham.

Page 17. Rev. Theron Brown, author of the "Epic of Windham", is a brother, not a son of John A. Brown of Mt. Hope. Their father was the late Eliphalet Brown.

Pages 18-19. The list of invited guests was copied from the Willimantic "Journal", and no attempt made to secure a fuller list.

Page 46, line 1, read 1825, instead of 1824; line 7, 1828 instead of 1827; Deacon Charles Lee built only two of the houses of the present Smithville White row, Gen. L. E. Baldwin the others.

Page 50, hanging of Watkins Aug. 31, 1832, instead of 1829.

Page 51, line 2. Gen. Amos Fowler is not living, but died in Windsor in 1876. It is his brother, Gen. Anson Fowler, who is now living in Lebanon.

Page 58. The H. P. & F. R. R. reached Willimantic from Hartford in 1849, and was opened to Providence in 1853.

Page 64, line 7, read Sumter instead of Richmond.

Page 65, read Jas. Haggerty enlisted at 14 (not 13) years, 1 mo. 11 days.

Page 78. William B. Swift, son of Grant Swift of Mansfield, started a little one-story silk mill on the site of the present west mill of the Holland Co., and the Hollands bought him out. Albert Jacobs built the brick house occupied by J. H. Holland, now by the Misses Brainard.

Pages 80-81. The Abolition disturbance occured in the spring of 1837, and the name of the leader of the mob was Charles Scoville, instead of Schofield. It was Edwards (not Edward) Clark who read the riot act.

Page 83. Samuel Bingham was cashier of the Windham Bank when it was robbed, James Parsons was teller and slept in the building.

Page 84, read Charles Smith of Smith, Winchester & Co., in his 85th. year, instead of 80th.

Page 87. The first newspaper published in Willimantic was the Windham "Gazette", and Elisha Avery has copies of it now in his possession. The "Public Medium" came later. At the Willimantic "Journal" office to-day may be seen the original woodcut of the headline of the "Public Medium", which represented a view of the Windham, Smithville and Jillson mills, and the river.

Page 89. The first physician of Willimantic was Dr. Mason. He came in 1827, and his wife's mother Mrs. Lambert, built in 1828 a house on the site of the present Dime and National bank building. Dr. Mason remained only three or four years and Dr. Witter was the first long-resident physican.

Page 138. The Jackson street lands were never owned by the colored man, whose name was Lyman Jackson, though long occupied by him and named from him. The late Eli Hewitt bought the property of Edwin Eaton of Chaplin and his daughter, Miss Mary A. Hewitt of South Windham now holds the deed.

THE COLLECTION OF RELICS.

At the time of the Bi-Centennial the press of Connecticut and neighboring states made note of event in interesting reports. The following appreciative comment of the Norwich correspondent of the New York *Sunday Tribune* is worthy of preservation, especially for its account of the very valuable collection of relics, whose articles are of course still to be found scattered among the families to whom they are credited in the list elsewhere printed in this volume:

"Norwich, June 11, 1892 (Special to the *Tribune*).—At the celebration at Windham Green this week of the town of Old Windham's 200th birthday anniversary a collection of ancient relics and family heirlooms was displayed in the Old Windham Bank that was never equalled by a similar private exhibition in the history of Connecticut. Two rooms in the building were lined with antique articles, all of which belong to residents of the town and are invaluable. Notable in the collection were immense full-length family portraits, 150 years old, whose canvas was time-stained and split in half a dozen places. The central portrait was not less than six feet tall. It depicted a lady of the old-fashioned type in the most highly starched pose, and in her lap a babe only a trifle less wooden of posture. It is an interesting fact that the infant in the picture became the mother of a respected citizen of Old Windham, who is still living at the age of ninety-two years. Another valuable heirloom was the continental uniform of Captain Larrabee, torn by the bullets with which he was desperately wounded in an Indian fight near Lake Champlain, in New York. A great old chest, exquisitely carved, that had not a nail mark in its frame, and was black with age, bore on its front the date, indented with a knife, 1696. There were a hundred other things almost equally precious. The village of Windham is rich in history. Most of its stately houses were built before the Revolution and are famous for their historical or legendary associations. In the Staniford Tavern, which is now the private home of the Elderkin family, Washington was quartered on several of his visits to Eastern Connecticut. The place was old when it sent troopers to join the Continental Army, and the French contingent of Washington's Army came there, led by gallant noblemen. The old sign of the Staniford Inn, belonging to the time of the British regime, is still as good as new, and swings above the door of the Old Windham Hotel, which is almost as old as the Staniford Tavern. An equally interesting relic is a wooden and highly-painted image of Bacchus, the property of A. E. Brooks, of Hartford, that was mounted at the Staniford Tavern. It was carved by prisoners of war, taken from the British vessel Bomrig, in Long Island Sound, in the Revolution, who were confined at the time in the Old Windham Jail. There is only one other figure of the kind in the country."

NOTE.—The statement that the Staniford Tavern is "now the private home of the Elderkin family", is an error on the part of the "Tribune" correspondent. The old Staniford Tavern was torn down, and the residence now occupied by Thomas Ramsdell was built on the same site.

INDEX.

[This index lays no claim to completeness of topics or symmetry of classification, but aims only to include, for convenience in reference, names and principal topics. It is believed that every family name to be found in the book has been indexed.—A. B. L.]

Abbe, typical family, 28.
    Chas. Smith, 17, 121, 122.
    Elisha, 41.
    George, 67.
    house, 15.
    Joshua, 53.
Abbee, Captain of the craft "Windham," 106.
    Richard, first County Treasurer, 30; opens first hotel, 31.
Abbeeites, 53.
Abimelech Sachem, 22.
Abolition Agitation, 80.
Academy at South Windham, 59.
Academy at Windham, 41.
Adams, A. B., 136.
    Elizabeth, 24.
    Joseph, 30.
    Samuel G., 130.
Adams Express Agency, 89.
Adams Nickel Plating Co., 75.
Adgate, Thomas, 21.
Air Line Railroad, 58.
Alcohol, Victims of, 57, 81.
Alderman, Rev. A. P., 54.
Alford, F. H., 88.
    G. H., 9, 132.

Alger, Gen., 65.
Allen, Amos Dennison, 61.
    Edwin, 73, 74.
    Henry, 19.
Allen, typical family, 28.
Alpaugh & Hooper, 133.
American Wood Type Co., 75.
Amherst, Lord, at Montreal, 35.
Amidon, Samuel E., 6.
Andrews, Rev. 51.
Andross, Sir Edmund, 21.
Anketell, Rev. John H., 52.
Archambeault's store, 132.
Arnold, Joel R., 64, 131, 134.
    Mrs. Julia, 9.
Ashley, Rev. R. K., 56.
Ashton, Thomas, 5, 12.
"At Home," poem, 108-9.
Atkinson, Edward, 77.
Atlanta Exposition, 77.
Attanwanhood, Joshua, son of Uncas, 20, 22, 97.
Atwood Block, 54, 80.
    Warren, 89, 130, 135.
Avery, Elisha, 148.
    Henry W., 60.
Babcock, typical family, 28
Babcock, Courtland, 132.

Bacchus, image 15, 43, 81.
Backus, typical family, 28.
    Ebenezer, 32.
    George H., 6.
    John, 23.
    William, 22, 23, 28.
    William C., 6.
Badger, typical family, 28.
    Daniel, 99.
    Edmund, 67, 68.
Bailey, James N., 130.
Baker, Mrs. Chas., 9.
    Chas. L., 64.
    Col. Rufus L., 63.
Baldwin, Jerome B., 6, 65.
    John, 91.
    Gen. Lloyd E., 3. 5, 6, 8, 15, 49, 50, 58, 85, 91, 129, 130, 133, 134, 141, 147.
Baptist church, 51, 52, 54, 55, 57, 136.
Barber, W. J., 87.
Barlow, Elder J. L., 57.
Barrows, Fred F., 60.
    Samuel, 134.
    Samuel Jr., 49.
Barstow, Wm. P., 9.
Bartlett, Reuben S., 19.
Bass, typical family, 28; of Scotland, 114.
Bassett, Joseph C., 4, 9, 84, 131.
Batrachian Battle, Windham's great, 32 and fol.
Beach, Frank E., 88.
Beckwith, Willard, 15.
Beebe, Rev. E., 54.
Beede, Frank H., 61.
Belair, Moses, 6.
Bell, Rev. Edward, 54.
Bennett, Origen, 4, 9.

Bennett, Perry, 61.
    Dr. William A., 65.
Bently, Dr. Eleazer, 60.
    Rev. E. D., 54.
Bibbins, typical family, 28.
Bi-Centennial Anniversary, 3.
Bill, Arthur I., 6, 8, 88.
    Eleazer, 131.
    Rev. F. W., 54.
    Horatio N., 5, 9.
Billings, typical family, 28.
Bingham, typical family, 28.
    Jonathan, 29.
    Miss Josie, 9.
    Roger, 53,
    Samuel, 148.
    Waldo, 4, 5, 8.
Birchard, John, 21.
Bissell, Hezekiah, 75.
Blanchette, J. Octave, 6.
Blish Frank H. 6, 61; of Perkins & B., 135.
Bliven Chas. S., 4, 137.
    Joseph B., 4.
Bolles John, 65.
Boon block, 91.
Boon, William C., 49, 134.
Borough of Willimantic, 49.
Boss, Charles L., 6,
    Eugene S., 3,
    Harry, 4, 8, 130.
Boston Ht'f'd & Erie R. R., 59.
Bowen, Chas. D., 64.
    Dr. Geo. Austin, 18.
Bowman, John, 5.
Bradford, Abel, 134.
    Rev. E. B., 54.
    Governor, 24.
Bradshaw, John T., 6.
Brady, Rev. Father H., 55.
Brainard, Henry, 59, 135.

Brainard house, 135.
   Misses, 78, 147.
Braley, Lester E., 64.
Branch, Wm., 128.
Brewster, Rev. Geo. W., 54.
   Rev. Joseph, 52.
   Sidney, 137.
Brick manufacture, 90.
Brigham, Walter D., 6.
Broderick, Dennis F., 6.
Bromley, Dr. Calvin, 60.
   Rev. Henry, 54.
   Stephen, 131.
Brooklyn, 44.
Brooks, Abel E., 6, 8, 15, 43, 149.
Brown, typical family, 28.
   Elder Harry, 57.
   Eliphalet, 147.
   John, 4, 8, 85, 91.
   John A., 17, 147.
   Lucius and wife, 19.
   Robert, 47, 86.
   Theron, 17, 65, 147.
Buck, Edwin A., 5, 49.
   Rev. Geo., 57.
Bugbee, J. Calhoun, 5.
Bull, George, 137.
Bunker Hill, 35, 36.
Burdick, Wm. L., 61.
Burleson, Allen B., 131.
Burlingham, Samuel L., 5, 78.
Burnham, typical family of Scotland, 114.
   Abel R., 130.
   Alfred A., 91.
   Chester, 18.
   Edward L., 4.
   Edwin E., 3, 4, 9.
   Elisha, 130.
   Geo. W., 4, 6, 8, 57.
   Henry, 9.
   Marvin, 4, 8.
Burnside, Gen., 65.

Bushnell, Serg't Richard, 22.
Button, Linden T., 4.
Byrne, George, 140.
   Smith and B., 140.
Cadwell, George A., 61.
Cady, Rev. Jonathan, 54.
Calkins, Hugh, 22, 124.
Cambridge, settlers from, 27.
Campbell, Miss Bertie 9, of New York, 140.
   Fred, 130.
   Jefferson, 130.
   Thomas, 91, 130.
Camp Ground M. E., 55.
Canada Parish, 27.
Canadian Immigration, 92-3.
Capen, Chas. A., 6, 8.
   homestead, 139.
   John H. 50, 139.
   Jillson & Capen, 92.
Card block, 91.
   David C., 6, 134.
Carding Machines, 45.
Carey, Eleazer, 30.
   Henry, 4.
   house, 139.
   John F., 6.
   typical family 28; of Scotland, 114.
   Samuel, 25.
   Waldo, 84.
Cargell, William C., 4, 89, 130.
Carpenter Bros., 84, 132.
   Chas. E., 6, 8.
   James H., 134.
   Loring, 49, 139.
Carroll, Charles, of Carrollton, 13.
   Rev. S. J., 55.
Carter, John, 67.
"Case Knife," Old Slave, 90.
Casey, Edward F., 6, 91, 140.

Cates, John, 15, 17, 23, 97, 98.
Catholics 11, 54, 56, 61, 92, 138.
Catlin, George S., 82, 91.
Chaffee, J. Dwight, 5.
    O. S. & Son, 78.
    Zelotes, 137.
Challenger, Geo., 5, 8, 9, 15.
Chamberlain family, 139.
    Prof. L. P., 9.
Chandler, Thomas C., 5, 129.
Chaplin, 4, 9.
Chapman, Amos S., 9.
    Horace M., 5.
Chappell, Herbert R., 6.
Charlestown, settlers from, 27.
Chase, George H., 7, 86.
    Laban, 86, 132.
Cheshire, 52.
Chipman, John, 137.
    Martha, 60.
Church, Rev. A. J., 55.
Churches of Windham, 51 and fol.
"Cindy," old slave, 90.
Clap, Rev. Thos., 24, 25, 26.
Clark, Abel, 137.
    Rev. Edgar F., 54.
    Edwards, 81, 147.
    Huber, 6.
    John G., 61.
    Lucian H., 139, 140.
    Silas F., 4.
    Maxon G., 139.
    Gen. Waterman C., 140.
    typical family, 28.
Clark & Gray, 45, 140.
Cleveland, typical family, 28.
    Edward S., 4, 16.
    President Grover, 52
    Rev. R. F., 51.

Cogswell, J. R., 19.
    Rev., 51.
Coker, Rev. M. G., 54.
Colgrove, Dr. C. H., 5, 137.
Collins, John, 87.
Colored population, 92.
Conant, Albert A., 4.
Congdon, Thomas R., 84,
Congregational church, 51, 52, 53, 81, 133.
Congressmen from Windham, 91.
"Connecticut Home" newspaper, 88.
Cook, Rev. Benajah, 54.
Cooley, John G., 34.
Cooper, Rev. John, 54.
Corbin, David P., 61.
Corson, Rev. L. H., 52.
County seat removed, 44.
Crampton, Rev. Ralph S, 53.
Crandall, W. C., 88.
Crane, Edmund, 132.
    Jonathan, 23, 28, 29, 30, 34, 124.
    "Aunt Lucy" 132.
    typical family, 28.
Cranston, Allen L., 130.
    Earl, 131.
    William H., 130.
    place, 84.
Crimean War, 75.
Crofts, Rev. C. P., 53.
Crown Point, 34.
Cunningham, Thos., 49, 133.
Curtis, Asa, 87.
    Rev. Wm. A., 52.
    Moseley, 91.
Cushman block, 136.
    E. McCall, 61, 136.
    J. E., 136.

Daniels, Charles N., 91, firm
of Grant & D., 68.
Dartmouth College, founded
by Windham man, 37.
David, Dr. Adelard D., 6, 12.
Davison, Capt. Calvin, 138.
Rev. G. K., 54.
Roderick, 4, 137, 138.
Day, Rev. Hiram, 52.
Dean, Josiah 84, 131.
Josiah, Jr., 131.
DeBruycker, Rev. Fl., 4, 11, 12, 13, 56.
Denison, typical family, 28.
Capt. George, 22.
Nathan, 33.
Deshon, Rev. Giles N., 52.
Devotion, typical family, 28;
of Scotland, 114.
family Bible, 16.
Devotion, Rev. Ebenezer, 25.
Ebenezer, Jr., 32.
Dewitt, Henry, 41.
Dexter, Stephen, 49.
Dido, story of Hettie's cosset, 77.
Dime Savings Bank, 83.
Dimmock, typical family, 28.
Dimock, Rose. 66.
Dingley, typical family, 28.
Dinsmore, Rev. C. A., 54.
Dodge, "Uncle Amos," 41.
Dorchester, Rev. Daniel, 54.
Dow, Lorenzo, 53.
Dowling, Rev. Thos., 54.
Dunham hall, 56; D. and Ives firm, 76.
Leonard R., 61.
Dunn, Daniel P., 6.
Durkee, Fort, 33.

Durkee, Capt. John, 33.
typical family, 28.
D., Stiles & Co., 136.
Dwight, Rev. Moseley, 54.
Dyer, typical family, 28.
Dr. Benjamin, 41.
Col. Eliphalet, 31, 33, 34, 36, 37, 41, 83, 103.
Mansion, 14, 15.
"Old Prime," slave, 70.
Thomas, 33.
Early Willimantic, 44.
Easter, Rev. A. Ogden, 52.
Eaton, Edwin, 148.
Eddy, Rev. Clayton, 52.
Edgarton, Henry L., 6.
Educational tables, 74.
Edwards, Rev. Harry, 52.
Elderkin, typical family, 28.
mansion of, 15.
Bela, 25.
Col. Jedediah, 31, 32, 36, 37, 41, 78, 83, 103.
E. & Wales firm, 36.
Joshua, Vine and John, 25.
Joshua, 15, 36.
Vine, 33.
Electric Light Co., 80.
Ellery, John, 25.
Elliott, Geo. C., 133.
English origin of population, 92.
"Enterprise" newspaper, 88.
Epic of Windham, The, 95.
Episcopal Society, 52, 56.
Essex, Wm. F., 133.
Evans, John, Charles and Edward, 87.
Rev. P. S., 54.
Everest, Rev. Cornelius B., 17, 51.

Exchange Place, 57, 141.
Faribault plan, 62.
Favroe, Arthur P., 4.
Feldman, L. and H., 133.
Fenn, Rev. W. A., 54.
Fenton, Capt. Chas, 65.
    I. P., 9.
    Palmer, 4.
First National Bank, 83.
First Settler, The, poem, 110.
Fish, Angeline, 132.
    Nathan, 132.
Fitch, Col. Ebenezer, 24.
    Edwin S., 50.
    Capt. Eleazer, 34, 35.
    Governor, 100.
    Hardin, 4, 9, 58, 84, 129.
    Dr. Jabez, 59.
    Rev. James, 21.
    Major James, 21.
    Capt. John, 34.
    Joseph, 24.
    Marcy, 33.
    Dr. Newton, 49, 135.
    tavern, 22.
    typical family, 28.
Fitches, mention of, 22.
Fitzpatrick, Patrick, 6.
Fletcher, Rev. Daniel, 54.
Flint, typical family, 28.
    Jairus, 32.
    Lucius Y., 4.
Flynn, Luke 6, 138.
    Luke, Jr., 138.
Follett's Pond, 96.
Follett, typical family, 28.
Ford, Samuel B., 132.
Foster, J. H., 88.
Foster & Post firm, 67.
Fourdrinier Brothers, Henry and Lealy, 70.
Fourdrinier Machines, 67-70.

Fowler, Major Gen. Amos, 50, 147.
    Amos T., 6.
    Gen. Anson, 147.
    Frank S., 137.
Fox, Chas. J., 3, 5, 6.
Franklin Hall, 55, 61, 85, 133.
Free, Rev. S. R., 53.
Freeman, Lucian, 4.
French Canadians, 5, 6, 92.
French and Indian War, 24.
French Mills, battle of, 63.
Frink, typical family, 28.
    Andrew, 8.
    Levi, 132.
    L. G., 9.
Frogs, Story of Windham, 32 and fol.; battle of, 100.
Frost & Pickering firm, 67.
Fuller, Deacon A. H., 54, 131.
    Jane Gay, 18, 110.
    L. J. and Son, 134.
    Thomas Hart, 61.
    typical family of Scotland, 114.
Fulsome, Israel and wife, 26.
Future, The, 93 and fol.
Gager, Edwin B., 17, 112.
    John P., 4.
    Lewis, 17.
    William, 24.
Gallows Hill, 31.
Gardner, Rev., 54.
Gates, Rev. Alfred, 54.
    Andrew F., 18.
    William F., 137.
Ginne, Joe, 23.
Ginnings, Jonathan, 23.
Godfrey, William, 138.
Gold Fever, 91.
Good Samaritan Movement, 82.

Gordon Place, 138.
Gould, Rev. John B., 54.
Governor's Foot Guards, 7.
Grant & Daniels firm, 68.
Gray, typical family, 28, 103.
    Clark and G., 146.
    Col. Ebenezer, 25, 37.
    John H., 133.
Green, Alonzo B., 131.
    Rev. Philetus, 54.
Greenslit, David A., 4, 9.
Gregory, Rev. Alva, 54.
Griggs, David A., 4.
    John, 9.
    Miss Nellie M., 16.
Grove Seminary, 59.
Guild, Dr. F. E., 9, 15, 147.
Gurley, Capt. Roger, 137.
Haggerty, James, 6, 65, 147.
Hale, Nathan, drum corps, 15.
Hall, Edwin H., 35, 131.
    E. H. Jr., 68.
    E. H. and Son, 86.
    Egbert, 132.
    H. & Bill Printing Co., 88.
    Henry, 50, 91.
    Henry L. 87.
    Horace, 61, 87, 91, 133.
    Hon. John M., 3, 5, 6, 7, 8, 87, 131, 133.
    Nathan, 132.
Hallam, Rev. Dr., 56.
Hammond, Elisha G., 4, 8.
    Lucius J., 5, 9, 14.
Hampton, 4, 9, 16, 27.
Hanlon, James E., 6.
Hanover Block, 91, 136.
    Geo. W., 136.
Haran, Thos., 133.
Hartford, Providence & Fishkill R. R., 58, 147.

Harrington house, 133.
Harris, Martin, 59, 141.
Harrison, Wm. Henry, 63, 80.
Hartson, Albert, 4, 8.
    Lester M., 6, 9.
Haskins, Rufus T., 5.
Hatch, Charles, 15.
    Henry, 9, 122.
    Mrs. Henry, 9.
    Jonathan, 4, 8.
Hatheway, Amos L., 17, 116.
    A. Morris, 17.
Hawkins, Wm. B., 50.
Hawthorne House, 139.
Hay Scales, 141.
Hayden, James, 3.
    Whiting, 46, 57.
Heap, Geo. P. 132, 136.
"Hearsay," by C. S. Abbe, 121 and fol.
Hebard, Geo. W., 91.
    Tavern, 50, 81, 91, 131.
    typical family, 28.
Hendee, Richard, 23.
Henney, John, 65.
Henry, John J., 6.
"Herald," newspaper, 34, 40, 86, 87, 88.
Herrick, Ephraim, 54, 139.
Hettie, Story of Cosset Dido, 77.
Hewitt Eli, 148.
    Miss Mary A., 148.
    Property, 138.
Hickey, John, 4, 138.
High School, 61.
Hill, Samuel L., 60.
Hills, T. Morton, 5.
Hine, Roderick W., 61.
"Hither Place," 23.
Holbrook, S. T., 19.
    Wm. A., 61.

157

Holden, Rev. C. W., 55.
  Rev. F. A., 52.
Holland, Dr. J. G., 78.
  J. H. & G., 78, 147.
Holland Manufacturing Co., 78.
Holman, Rev. Geo. W., 54.
Holmes, Elisha, 75.
  E. Harlow, 5, 8, 9.
  Mrs. Sarah, 9.
Holt, Geo. M., 9.
Hooker, S. Chauncey, 6.
  House, 49, 53.
Hooper's Lane, 86.
Hooper, Alpaugh and H., 135.
  Robert, 132.
Hopley, Rev. Samuel, 52.
Horbush, Rev. H , 54.
Horseshoe Bridge built, 43.
Horton, Rev. S. J., 15, 16, 52.
Hosmer, James D., 130.
  Mountain, 48.
  Stephen, 48, 49, 130.
  Wm. H., 89, 91, 130.
Hovey, Rensalaer O., 50.
  Judge, 89.
Howes, Alfred, 135.
  James, 136.
  blacksmith shop, 47.
Hoxie, Benjamin B. 4.
Hoyt, F. K., 9.
Hubbard, Amos H., 71.
Hudson, Henry, 71.
Huguenot Descendants, 114.
Hunter, John L., 5, 131.
Huntington, Charles, 59.
  Major Hezekiah, 36.
  Joseph, 23, 30.
  Nathaniel, Enoch, Jos. and Jabez, 25.
  Jabez, 30.

Huntington, Rufus, 48.
  Samuel, 36-7, 40.
  Simon, 21, 22.
  Thomas, 30.
  typical family, 28; of Scotland, 114.
Hunt, typical family, 28.
Hyde, William, 21.
"Independent Observer and County Advertiser," newspaper, 87.
Indian charity school, 37.
Ingersoll, Jared, 35.
Ireland, Archbishop, 62.
Irish population, 92.
Iron ore, 28.
Iron Works, 28, 36.
Iron Works Bridge, 47.
Ives, Dunham & I., firm 76.
Jackson, Gen. Andrew, 85.
  Lyman, 138, 148.
  Street, 55, 56.
Jacobs, Ward W., 4.
Jefferson, Rev. H. B., 57.
Jennings, Jonathan, 99.
  Joseph, 31.
  Royal, 49.
  typical family, 28.
Jewett, Charles, 9.
  Mrs. Chester, 9.
Jillson, Asa, 49, 131.
  Bros., (Wm., Asa and Seth,) 45.
  Mill, 75.
  J. and Capen, 76, 92, 139, 140.
  Capt. John S., 50.
  Seth, 131.
  William C., 3, 6, 131, 140.
  Capt. William L., 50, 85.
  William, 137.
  Col. William, 131, 140.

Johnson, Mrs. Ann H., 15.
  Merrick, 137.
  Sir William, 24.
  Rev. William, 34.
Johnson's livery stable, 134, new block, 135.
Jordan, Chas. B., 6, 60.
  Lyman, 48, 130.
  Thomas, 130.
"Journal," Willimantic, 9, 11, 14, 18, 87.
Judson, Rev. Philo, 53.
Keigwin, John G., 3, 5, 6, 84, 133.
Keith, Rev. O. F., 52.
Kellen, Rev. William, 54.
Kelley, Thos. J., 3, 5, 9.
Kellogg, Eunice Richmond, 132, 135.
Kelsey, Rev. W. S., 52.
Kennedy, typical family, 28.
Kenyon, Miss Emma, 9.
  E. P., 9.
Killourey, John, 138.
Kimbel, Block, 133.
  Stephen, 133.
King family, 131.
Kingsburys, typical family, 28.
Kingsley, Dr. 139.
  Wm. 60.
  typical family of Scotland, 114.
Knapp, Rev. Henry R., 54.
LaFayette, Gen. 12.
Lamnon, Wm. C., 19.
Land values, 49, 89.
La Palme, J. Godfrey, 4.
Larned, Miss Ellen D., 18.
Larrabee, Capt. Adam, 62, 63.
  Charles, 4, 8, 19, 63.
  Chas., Jr., 6, 8, 9.

Larrabee, Major Chas., 62, 63.
  Miss Emma, 9.
  Henry, 3, 5, 8, 19, 43, 63.
  Mrs. Henry, 9.
  John 23.
  Timothy, 42, 44, 63.
  typical family, 28
  William, 9.
Latham, Wm. H., 5.
Lathrop, Azariah, 132.
  Charlotte, 15.
  Dr., 64.
  Elder Benjamin, 53.
  George, 4, 5, 8, 9, 140.
  H. Clinton, 6, 8, 9.
  Jabez, 5, 61.
  James P., 19.
  Mrs Lee, 16.
  typical family, 28.
Law students, 89.
Leader, Rev. Shadrach, 55.
Leavitt, Rev. D. P., 55.
  N. W., 88.
Leavitt's operetta, 90.
Lebanon, 26, 27.
Lee, Deacon Chas., 46, 48, 52, 132, 147.
Leffingwell, Lieut. Thos., 21, 22.
Lemon, Rev. J. B., 54.
Leonard, Chas. E., 6.
  Rev. S., 54.
  Zephaniah, 25.
Lester, Hannah G., 63.
  John F., 58.
Levingworth and Wells firm, 74.
Lewis, Prentiss, 9.
  Sheffield, 135.
Lexington, 36.
Liberty meetings, 35.

Lincoln, Allen, 17, 47.
  Allen B., 3, 5, 6, 9, 17, 39, and fol., 88, 129.
  Edgar S., 5, 59.
  Frank M., 4, 5, 9.
  George, 131.
  John C. 6.
  Lorin, 4, 9.
  M. Eugene, 3, 5, 6.
  Stowell, 68.
  typical family, 28.
Linen Co., 75.
Little, Saxton B., 61.
Littlefield, Jairus, 134.
Livesey, Rev. John, 64.
Locke, Wm. H., 54.
Lockman, DeWitt, 9.
Long, Francis S., 64.
Loomer, Silas, 3, 5, 91.
  Vilatia, 137.
Loomer's lumber yard, 138.
Loomis, Andrew, 64.
  Mrs. Eliza, 9.
  Mrs. Lavinia, 134.
Lord, Daniel, 135.
  Joshua B., 85, 91, 135.
  Marian, 135.
Loring, A. D. 4, 9, 45.
  Solomon, 45.
Lynch, Jas. T. 3, 5, 82.
Lyon, Gen. Nathaniel, 65.
  Guards, 64.
Magoon, Isaac, 27, 114.
Manahan, Geo. W., 130.
Manning, typical family, 28
Mansfield, 4, 9, 24, 27, 28.
Martin, typical family, 28.
  James, 130.
  Deacon Luther, 131.
  J. Griffin, 5, 8, 9.
Mason, Daniel, 21.
  Capt. John, 20, 21, 22.

Mason, John, 124.
  Samuel, 21, 22.
Masons, mention of, 22.
Massachusetts Bay, settlers from, 27.
May, Rev. Geo., 54.
Mayflower, The, 24.
McAvoy, James A., 5. 137.
McBurney, Rev. S., 55.
McCabe, Rev. Bernard, 55.
McCracken, Geo. B., 131.
McDonald, John A., 6, 88.
McFarland, Bishop, 56.
McManus, Gen. Thomas, 13.
McReading, Rev. Chas. S., 54.
McQuade, Bishop, 56.
Melony, block, 53, 133.
  George W., 5.
  Norman, 4, 48.
Memorial building, 7, 8.
Merchants Loan & Trust Co., 83.
Merrick Bros., 6, 8.
Merrill, Chas. F., 61.
Merrow, Joseph B., 5.
Methodists, 54, 55, 80, 135.
Militia, state, 50.
Millard, typical family, 28.
  Benjamin, 29.
Miller, Rev. George W., 55.
  Samuel J., 64, 65.
Miner, Rev. Cyrus, 54.
Monast, Joseph E., 6.
Montgomery Hose Co., 11.
Montreal, surrender of, 35.
Morrill, Principal A. B., 12.
Morris, Jonathan Flint, 18.
Morrison, Albert R., 5.
  John H., 6.

Morrison, Henry, 79.
W. G. & A. R. Machine Co., 79.
Walter G., 79.
William, 130.
Morse, Rev. Charles H., 54.
Moulton, typical family, 28.
Albert R., 4, 138.
Everett H., 3, 5, 9.
George S., 40.
Harriet, 60.
Edward, 140.
Rev. Horace, 54.
John H., 3, 5, 6, 58, 131, 137.
Col. Roswell, 91, 131.
William, 4.
Mullen, Rev. Daniel, 56.
Murdoch, typical family, 28.
Murray, Hugh C., 5.
James E., 3, 5, 6, 138.
Nason, George K., 6.
Natchaug school building, 60.
Silk Company, 78.
Nesbitt, George F., 73.
Nesbitt's wood type, 73.
New Boston, 67.
"New England Home" newspaper, 9, 88.
New Haven, Middletown and Willimantic R. R., 59.
New England Township, Its History and Mission, 116 and fol.
New London Northern R. R., 58.
"News" Willimantic daily, 88.
Newspapers of Willimantic, 86 and fol.
Newton, settlers from, 27.
New Village, 76.

New York and New England R. R., 59.
Ney, John M., 18.
Nichols, Rev. Abel, 52.
Nipmuck Path, 15.
Indians, 20.
Noble, Rev. Charles, 54.
Non-consumption ordinance, 35.
Normal Training school, 61.
North and South Windham, 67 and fol.
North Windham manufactures, 67 and fol.
Oaks, The, 76.
Obwebetuck, 38.
Ohio Reservation, 34.
Oldest houses in town, 84.
Old stone school house, 58, 61, 139, 140.
Old Windham, 40 and fol.
Old Windham of to-day, 82 and fol.
Olmstead, John, 21, 22.
O'Reilly, Rev. Father Hugh J., 56.
Ormsby, typical family, 28.
Osborn, Wm. H., 46, 137.
Otis, Dr. Wm. K., 136,
Page, E. S., 131.
Henry, 4, 8.
P. & Son, 140.
Palmer, typical family, 28; of Scotland, 114.
Rev. A. P., 55.
Wm. F., 49.
Parochial School, 56, 61.
Patriotic address issued, 35.
Peabody, G. B., 9.
Mrs. G. B., 9.

Pearl, Patrick H., 4.
Peck, Pearl L., 50.
Perkins, typical family, 28.
    P. & Blish, 135.
    Emeline L., 19.
    John A., 4, 8, 15, 135.
    Miss Mary, 9.
Perry, Albert L., 4, 8.
Peters, historian and parson, 32, 100.
Phelps, Aaron, 80.
    James, 70.
    P. & Spafford, firm, 71.
Philip, King, 21.
"Phoenix" newspaper, 34.
Pickering, Englishman, 67.
    Joseph, 70.
Pierce, Timothy, 30.
Pierson, Walt, 87.
Pigeon Swamp, 69.
Pinney, Julius, 5.
Plains, The, 50.
Platt, Dennis, 53.
Plattsburg, 63.
Polling places, 46.
Pomeroy, Chas B., 6.
Pondes, The, 23.
Population, 41, 92.
Porter, Miss Sarah, 130.
Post, William, 130.
Post, John, 22.
Post, of Foster & Post firm, 67.
Potter, Niles, 91, 133.
    William N., 6.
Potvin, Theodore, 5.
Powder Mills, 36.
Powell, Principal, 61.
Preliminary Efforts for Bi-Centennial, 3.
Prentice, Robert, 132.
Presbyterian Church, 53.

Progressive Lyceum, 57.
Protestants, 61.
"Public Medium" newspaper, 87.
Purington, Rev. Wm,, 54.
Purinton, Geo. H, 5.
Putnam Phalanx, 7.
Quinn, Rev. Father J. J., 13.
Railroads, The, 57.
Raisley, Rev. J. E., 54.
Ramsdell, Rev. H., 54.
    Thomas, 8, 43.
Ransom, Rev. Reuben, 54.
Rathbun, Elias, 132.
    Julius G., 4, 18.
Reading Coal Co., 58.
"Record", daily newspaper, 88.
Reed, typical family, 28.
    E. F,, 130.
    Rev. George E., 55.
Reform Church and Society, 57.
Reforms, Windham in, 80.
Rehoboth, settlers from, 27.
Relics, Exhibition of, 142 and following.
Remington, Homer E., 6.
Revolution, Windham in the, 35 and following.
Richardson, Leander, 60.
Richmond, Perez O., 45.
Rifle Company, 50.
Ripley, typical family, 28.
    Brothers, 64.
    Eleazer H., 64.
    Hezekiah, 25.
    Jeremiah, 23.
    Joshua, 23, 30.
    Joshua D., 30.
    Nehemiah, 31.

Risley, Oliver H. K., 5.
Robbery of Windham Bank 83.
Robbins, typical family, 28.
   Miss Josephine M., 16, 108.
Robert, Louis, 70.
Robinson, typical family, 28; of Scotland, 114.
   Rev. A. 54.
   Andrew, 53.
   Calvin, 81, 139.
   Israel, 4, 9, 132.
   Mrs. J. C., 139.
   Luther, 138.
   Nathaniel, 138.
   Orrin, 81.
   Remus, 60.
   "Aunt Rushy", 81
Rogers, Frederic, 6.
   Rev. Geo. W., 54.
Rollinson, Joseph, 139.
Rood, Rufus, 8, 15.
Root, Thomas, 30.
Ross, James H., 6.
Rudd, typical family, 28.
Rust, Nathaniel, 30.

Safford, Addison, 139.
   Fayette, 88.
   Dr. Jason, 134.
Salem, settlers from, 27.
Saltonstall, mention of family, 24.
Saunders, Rev. E. W., 52.
Savings Institute, 82.
Sawyer, typical family, 28.
Scoville, Charles, 81.
Schools of Windham, 59 and following.
Scotch Presbyterian descendants, 114.

Scotland, 4, 9, 47, 112 and following.
Scott, John, 5, 131.
   Gen. Wihfield S., 63.
Searing, Rev. R. C., 56.
Sectaries, 43, 51.
Select School for boys, 52.
Separatist agitation, 26, 42,51.
Sessions, Daniel, 90.
Shad fishing, 43.
Sharpe, Rev. Andrew, 5, 53.
Shaw, Betty, execution of, 31.
Sherman, Rev. Henry B., 52.
Shoe Industry, 90.
Silk Manufacture, 32.
Simons, typical family, 20.
Simpson, C. S., 87.
Six Nations, The, 33.
Skiff, typical family, 28.
Slaves in Windham, 90.
Slavery abolished in Conn., 90.
Sliding Falls, 28.
Small Pox scourge, 84,
Smith, typical family, 28.
   A. D. and J. Y., (Governor), 46.
   Benajah, 12, 65.
   Charles, 4, 8, 71, 74, 84.
   C. M., 19.
   Captain David, 50.
   Guilford, 3, 5, 8, 15, 16, 74, 122.
   Mrs. Guilford, 9.
   James, 4, 8.
   John, 84, 139.
   Joshua, 69.
   "Pete" old slave, 90.
   Scott, 84, 139.
   William, 4, 15, 46, 59.
   S., Winchester & Co , 69, 72, 74, 75, 84.
   S. & Byrne, 140.

Smithville Co., 46, 80.
Snell, typical family, 28.
    Thomas, 29, 31.
Sodom, 81.
South Windham, 32, 52, 69 and following.
Southworth, typical family, 28.
Spafford, typical family, 28.
    George, 5, 68, 69, 70, 71, 72, 140.
    Henry, 4, 8.
    Jesse, 49.
Spaulding, Asa, 25.
Spencer, typical family, 28.
    Freeman D., 4, 8.
Spiritualists, 57.
Sprague, Gov., 65.
Stage coaches, 43.
St. Jean Baptist Society. 15.
St. Joseph's Roman Catholic Parish, 11,
Stamp Act, effect in Windham, 35.
Staniford, typical family, 28.
    Colonel, 62.
    Inn, 15, 43, 89.
Stanton, Robert, 9.
Starkweather, Ephraim, 25.
    Henry C., 4, 19.
    Nathan, 18.
Stearns, Rev. Geo. I., 17, 52.
Sterry, James, 132.
Stewart, Robert, 60.
Stiles, Geo. E., 6.
Stoddard, Allen, 91.
Stone, Edward, 130.
Storrs, Augustus, 4.
    William, 58.
Stubbs, Rev. Alfred H., 52.
Sullivan, Jeremiah O', 4, 5, 8.

Sumner, Elliott B., 5.
    Dr. E. G., 9.
Sumter, Fall of Fort, 64.
Susquehanna Company, 33.
Swan, Rev. Jabez, 51.
Swedes, 92.
Sweeney, Wm. J., 6.
Sweet, Stutely, 89.
Sweetland, Ira, 131.
Swift, Grant, 59.
    hill, 96.
    Mrs. Julia, 9.
    Justin, 46, 50, 68, 90.
    Rowland, 18.
    Storrs, 4.
    Zephaniah, 19, 40, 43, 89.
Taintor, typical family, 28,
    Chas., 67, 68, 89.
    John, 67.
    Henry E., 64.
    Mrs. Mary D., 9.
    T. Abbe & Badger, firm, 67.
Talcott, Hart, 18.
Tanner, Warren, 134.
Tarbox, Dr. Asahel, 120.
Taverns of Windham, 43.
Taylor, Geo. F., 5.
    Gen. Zachary, 63.
Teaming industry, 59.
Temperance Question, 57, 81 and following.
Temple street, 136.
Temple of Fashion, 136.
Terry, D. F., 130.
Tew, James, 86.
    John, 86.
    William, 86.
Thompson, Rev. Frank, 52.
Throop, Benjamin and William, 25.
    Dyer, 25.

Tiffany, George, 130.
Tighes, Jas., 6.
Tilden, Rev. Chester, 54, 134.
   Chester, Jr., 4, 9, 134.
   Marshall, 5.
Tingley, A. C., 129.
   T. & Watson, firm, 46.
   house, 131.
Tirrell, Rev. Eben, 55.
Todd, Rev. Charles, 52.
Toll-gate and house, 48, 130.
Townsend, Rev. P., 54.
Tracy, typical family, 28; of Scotland, 114.
   Lieut. Thos.
Training Days, 50.
"Transcript", newspaper, 87.
Tremont house, 133.
Trumbull, "Brother Jonathan," 28, 36.
Truscott, Robert, 132.
Turner, Albert S., 6.
   Arthur G., 5, 79, 89.
   Chauncey, 4, 130.
   Melancthon, 134.
   Thomas, 156.
   T. & Wilson, 84.
Turnpike Company, 42.
   Lines, 42.
Tyler, Rev. John, 51, 52.
Uncas, 20, 21.
Universalism, 17.
Universalist Church, 87, 140.
Utley, Chas. R., 6, 131.
   John R., 4.
Vaughn, Douglass, 138.
Verplanck, F. A., 61.
Vincent, Rev. Hebron, 54.
Wagons, 42.

Walden, typical family, 28.
   James, 3, 5, 7, 89, 91, 135.
   John L., 6.
Waldo, typical Scotland family, 114.
Wales, typical family, 28.
   Henry N., 91.
   Nathan, 33.
   Nathaniel, Jr., 36.
   William, 4, 8, 122.
Walworth, Reuben H., 63.
Ward, Rev. K., 54.
Warner house, 60.
Warner, typical family, 28.
Washburn, Edgar S., 5.
Washington, Gen., 14, 28, 36.
   Monument, 43.
Washingtonian movement, 82.
Waterman, Rev. Elijah, 51.
Watkins hanging, 50.
Weaver, Davis, 137.
   Elisha, 49.
   Thos. Snell, 9, 16, 20 and following, 87, 88, 137.
   William L., 16, 20, 60, 61, 87, 91, 133, 138.
Webb, typical family, 28; of Scotland, 114.
   Arthur B., 19.
   Frank F., 5, 8.
   Mrs. Frank F., 9.
   Henry, 87.
   Joel, 36.
   Joel W., 3, 5, 6.
   old family place, 15.
   Peter, 44.
   William, 91.
Webster, Chas. F., 61.
   Noah D., 6.
Welch, typical family, 28.
   John B., 61.

Wells, Rev. L. H., 56.
   of Levingsworth & W.
     firm, 74.
Welsh, Daniel, 25.
West, Ebenezer, 30.
Wetherell, Daniel, 22.
Wheat, Pasdon A. C., 54.
Wheeler, Rev. E. S., 54.
   George, 141.
   John D., 61, 131.
   Rev. L. W., 54.
Wheelock, Rev. Eleazer, D.
   D., 37.
White, typical family, 28.
   "Old Cruse" slave, 90.
   Rev. Moses, 80.
   Parson, 33.
   Rev. Stephen, 21, 51.
Whiting, typical family, 28, 99.
   Elizabeth, 24.
   John, 24.
   Rev. John, 24.
   Nathan, 35.
   Rev. Samuel, 24, 30, 34, 124.
   Samuel, Jr., 24, 34.
Whittemore Park, 138.
Wilkinson, Ahab, 139.
   Gen. 63.
   Joanna, 140-1.
Willard, Rev. S. G., 53, 130, 132.
Williams, A. B., 91.
   Arthur, 9.
   Elisha, 85, 139.
   Mrs. E. H., 19.
   Ralph, 130.
   Roger, 5.
   Wightman, 49, 132.
Willimantuck, first settlement, 23.
   In 1850, 139 and fol.

Willimantic Linen Co., 75.
   Newspapers, 86 and fol.
Wilson, of Turner & W. firm, 84.
   C. H., 9.
   Frank M., 5, 84, 135.
   Jesse, 137.
   Isaac, 134.
Winchester, Arthur S., 5, 9, 15.
   E. Clinton, 3, 5.
   Harvey, 72.
Windham, 4, 24, 29, 30, 44.
Windham Bank, 80, 83.
   Bank Robbery, 83.
   Churches, 51.
   County "Herald," 62.
   Green, 14, 28.
   Manufacturing Co., 46, 59, 79, 84, 91.
   in Reforms, 80.
   Schools, 59.
   The Coasting Vessel, 41, 106.
   in War, 62.
Windham's First Century, 20 and following.
Windham's Second Century, 39 and following.
Winslow, Rev. Horace, 4, 19, 50, 53.
Wiswall, Rev. F. M., 5.
Witter, Dr., 49, 85, 89, 132, 133.
   Wm. C., 4.
Wolcott, typical family, 28.
   Roger, 31.
Wood, Lieut. Chas., 64.
Wood type, 72.
Woodward, Dr. Ashbel, 66.
   Rev. John W., 52.
   Joseph, 137.
   P. H., 18, 66.
Woodworth, Chester, 9.
Wool, Gen., 65.

Wooster, Gen., 24.
Work, James H., 91,
Worth, Rev. Wm. T,, 55.
Wyoming Valley, 33-4.
Yale College, 24, 25, 31, 53.
Yergason, E. S., 9.
Yorktown, 35.
"Younger Generation", 116 and following.

Young, Alfred, 84, 131.
  Chas., 84.
  Frank A., 61.
  Fred S., 6.
  Henry, 138.
  Ulysses, 138.
Youngs hotel, 91, 133.

PRESS OF THE NEW ENGLAND HOME, HARTFORD.

www.ingramcontent.com/pod-product-compliance
Lightning Source LLC
Chambersburg PA
CBHW031445160426
43195CB00010BB/853